Hedda Sander/Björ

JUDO

from White/Yellow Belt to Brown Belt

Meyer & Meyer Sport

Aachen: Meyer und Meyer Verlag, 2001
Translated by James Beachus

British Library Cataloguing in Publication Data
A catalogue for this book is available from the British Library

Sander/Deling:
Judo – from White/Yellow Belt to Brown Belt.
Hedda Sander ; Björn Deling.
– Oxford: Meyer und Meyer, (UK) Ltd., 2002
ISBN 1-84126-076-2

All rights reserved, especially the right to copy and distribute, including the translation rights. No part of this work may be reproduced – including by photocopy, microfilm or any other means – processed, storedelectronically, copied or distributed in any form whatsoever without the written permission of the publisher.

© 2002 by Meyer & Meyer Sport (UK) Ltd.
Aachen, Adelaide, Auckland, Budapest, Graz, Johannesburg,
Miami, Olten (CH), Oxford, Singapore, Toronto
Member of the World
Sports Publishers' Association
www.w-s-p-a.org
Illustrations: Hedda Sander
Printed and bound by Druckerei Vimperk, AG
Cover Photo: Foto Design Agentur Volker Minkus, Isernhagen
ISBN 1-84126-076-2
E-Mail: verlag@m-m-sports.com
www.m-m-sports.com

JUDO

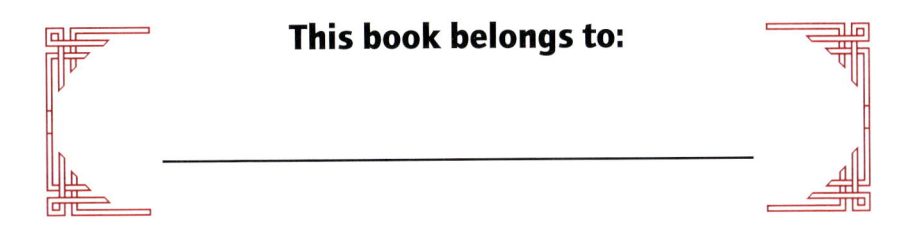

This book belongs to:

_____

Space for autographs:

CONTENTS

Foreword 9
1   Breakfall Techniques (Ukemi) – Forward, Backwards, Sideways . . . 13
2   Gripping Methods 17
3   Breaking the Grip/Developing Your Own Grip Style 19
4   Sequence Moves 21
    Pulling out Sequence 22
    Kodokan Sequence Rearwards 23
    Kodokan Sequence Forwards 24
    Straight Sequence 25
    Kawaishi Sequence 26
    Exercises 27
5   **Throwing Exercises** 31
    5.1 White/Yellow Belt 31
        O GOSHI 31
        O SOTO OTOSHI 33
        SASAE TSURI KOMI ASHI 35
        DE ASHI BARAI (Rearwards) 37
        DE ASHI BARAI (Forwards) 39
        A Judo-safari Story 41
    5.2 Yellow Belt 42
        O GOSHI (Sweeping Movement) 42
        KOSHI GURUMA 45
        SEOI OTOSHI 48
        KO UCHI GARI 50
        O UCHI GARI 52
        Winning by Giving-in 54
    5.3 Yellow/Orange Belt 56
        IPPON SEOI NAGE 56
        TSURI KOMI GOSHI 58
        TAI OTOSHI 60
        TAI OTOSHI (Straight Sequence) 62
        O SOTO GARI 64
        DE ASHI BARAI (Sweeping Movement) 66
        And Something about Competition Rules 68

CONTENTS

5.4 Orange Belt 70
   HARAI GOSHI 70
   KO SOTO GAKE 72
   O UCHI BARAI 74
   KO UCHI BARAI 76
   SASAE TSURI KOMI ASHI (Sweeping Movement) 78
   Practice Makes Perfect 80
5.5 Orange/Green Belt 82
   KO UCHI MAKI KOMI 82
   TOMOE NAGE 84
   YOKO TOMOE NAGE 88
   OKURI ASHI BARAI 91
   UCHI MATA (KOSHI) 93
   What Every Judoka Needs to Know 95
5.6 Green Belt 97
   TANI OTOSHI 97
   YOKO OTOSHI 99
   SUMI GAESHI 101
   HANE GOSHI 103
   The Belt Holds the Jacket Together 105
5.7 Blue Belt 106
   ASHI UCHI MATA 106
   O UCHI GARI (with Leg Reap) 108
   KATA ASHI DORI 110
   KUCHIKI TAOSHI 112
   USHIRO GOSHI 114
   UTSURI GOSHI 116
   TE GURUMA 118
   TE GURUMA (as a Counter) 121
   The Forms of Judo Exercises 123
5.8 Brown Belt 124
   ASHI GURUMA 124
   O GURUMA 126
   KATA GURUMA (Kneeling Shoulder Wheel) 129
   KATA GURUMA (Shoulder Wheel) 130
   SOTO MAKI KOMI 134
   URA NAGE 136
   YOKO GURUMA 139

CONTENTS

    Your Prospects 141
    5.9 More Throws. 143
        TSUBAME GAESHI 143
        YOKO SUMI GAESHI. 145
        KHABARELLI 146
        KOGA SEOI NAGE. 150
        YOKO GAKE 153

6   **The Throwing Circle** **155**

7   **Competition Card** **156**

8   **A Mini Japanese Vocabulary**. **157**

9   **Cut-out Pages for the Exercises** **161**

10   **Postscript** **166**

11   **Appendix: Stardust Answers to the Pixie's Questions**. **169**

FOREWORD

Dear Judo Kids,

During your training session, many of you have probably often asked your instructor, "How can I possibly remember all that? Don't you have notes, where it's all listed down what I have to learn to do a belt grading?"

Well, we sat down and thought through how we could put together a list like you want. We have mused over all the sort of questions you have asked and thought about the typical mistakes that happen.

It soon came clear that the result was something more than just a memory jogger for the next belt grading test. We found that even here pictures often spoke a thousand words, as the saying goes, and that photographs didn't always show all the important elements of a technique.

So we have filmed on video all the throws shown in this book, and from the film we have made **sketches** (just like in a cartoon) **with the Pixie and the Bear** as characters. These are there to demonstrate all the important points regarding a technique. TORI (the thrower) is always shaded dark, and UKE (the person being thrown) is not shaded-in. The important points are contained in the **balloons** around the characters.

Because we were often asked by many children how the feet should be placed for a particular throw, we have included the **step sequence** of where to place them for each of the techniques. This will assist you when trying to remember the individual throws.

A **detailed description** accompanies the sketches, however, for each technique there is **a little saying** – magical stardust formula from the Pixie's wand – to help you perhaps during the test when you have forgotten something.

The **little tests** are aimed at providing you with an aid to deepen your understanding for a technique, and to get you 'fit' for your grading test. If you can understand the test questions and answer them easily then you should have no problems later when doing the grading. Using the tests, you can give some thought later for which grip is best suited leading up to a throw and possible combination for further techniques. This can help you develop your own throwing circle.

FOREWORD

We have laid the book out so that, first of all, you will find the **basic techniques** (Judo breakfalls, the grips, breaking the grips, sequences). Descriptions in later techniques often build from these and if you have forgotten something you can easily and quickly find them again in the basics. The throws, which you have to know for the test, follow on from this and are laid out **in the order of the various belt grading**. As the belt grading requirements here are taken from the German grading system, grading requirements may differ slightly for you, if you live in another country. Don´t hesitate to ask your instructor about the technique you need to know for your next exam. They are mostly in here and you can look them up easily using the index! The description of each comes first and this is followed by the training exercises. Cut-out sheets, which you will need in order to memorize things, are at the end of the book. The answers to the little tests are in an Appendix – but first of all, you should try to answer the questions without looking them up. Finally, there is a section on 'More throws', which you don't absolutely need for the grading tests, but which are useful to know since you can use them successfully as techniques in competition. 'Groundwork' is not included in this book as this will be covered in a second volume.

So now you know enough to begin learning, but don't forget one thing: you can only learn Judo if you have the support of a patient partner **and practice again and again** under the guidance of your instructor. Just reading a book will not give you the necessary skill, which you need to carry out the various techniques described in the book. You should, also, always remember that you are **responsible** for your training partner – if he or she is suddenly injured, you can't practice any more. And if you ever have a question, turn to your trainer – he will most certainly help to clear up your point.

Have lots of fun learning

The little Pixie and the little Bear

FOREWORD FOR THE TRAINER

This book was written following the revision of the grading tests and because of the requirement to give children and also their parents exact information about the programme of belt gradings. They follow the requirements for the German grading system but can be easily adapted to the grading systems of other countries as they all require mostly the same skills and techniques, even if their successive order may slightly differ.

We wanted to encourage children to take an interest in their sport over and above the training sessions, and to create a better understanding for its complexities. In order to achieve interaction, the form of a **mimic and copy book**, for the deepening of understanding of the complex movements learned in instruction, was considered best. We have therefore put together training **exercise material on separate pages** for each of the illustrated throws, sequences, grips and breakfall techniques. The exercises are organised **according to age group** and can be easily carried out by children on their own. It is likely that the younger children will use the balloons in the comic sketches and the 'stardust' rhyming forms more, while the older ones will be more able to read the texts. We have laid out the throws down to the last detail so that children, who learn from pictures, will be able to visualise the movements also at home. In training and for the grading tests in the lower Kyu levels, one should be content that **the child, first of all, shows stamina and coordination ability as it gets very close to the optimum technique as "a form of"** or a "rough" achievement, as far as the grading test will allow. The training exercise material has been **tested** on all age groups over a period of two years or more by ourselves and several other instructors. On occasions the children worked on the exercises **on their own at home**, and at other times during the instruction periods, using prearranged methodical sessions or inductive methods. Naturally the children were given assistance and guidance on how UKE has to react in order to avoid mistakes being made by a rather anxious and tense partner as far as possible. We noticed a considerably higher **motivation** in children, who had actively gone through the exercise material. Their **participation in the instruction** was clearly stronger and as a result they did well in the grading test.

We wish the "stardust" seekers further "magical" success, and for all those who want to have a go with this mime and copy book, we hope the "wand" of luck will come their way.

Dr Hedda Sander and Björn Deling

FOREWORD FOR THE PARENTS

Dear Parents,

This book will perhaps help to inform you, what your children actually learn during their Judo instruction. Please also remember that it is **not only** about learning a complex series of movements in order to gain the next belt – quite the contrary, it's about the **development of the child's personality**. The necessary **stamina and development** of the child's coordination to be able to demonstrate the finer detail of certain techniques requires several years.

Simultaneously your child will learn **understanding and courtesy** for the partner with whom the child has to work closely together. He or she will also learn success and failure in a "Randori" (sparring training) and how to digest these and later make nothing of them. By coming to grips with these tasks, the **self-confidence** will gradually grow.

Take an interest in this development by reading about the lessons, and perhaps even encourage your child's progress, especially in the training test exercises, by also using this book.

Have fun together through the lessons
The Authors!

1 BREAKFALL TECHNIQUES

BREAKFALL TECHNIQUES 1

Breakfall techniques are necessary in order fall safely when you have been thrown. These techniques are also useful outside Judo when you fall down. You have to practice breakfalls again and again until you master falling down on both sides and until you can do the motions "blind-folded". Falls are divided into ones done backwards, left forwards, right forwards and sideways.

The breakfall techniques have two things in common:

Firstly, slap the mat hard with your arm stretched out next to your body (the elbow must not be bent otherwise you will hit the point of it on the ground). Doing this absorbs the shock of the fall. **Take care to slap the ground right next to your body** (two hand-widths away) so that you don't drop into the temptation of trying to support yourself with it, as this will jolt your shoulder.

Secondly, bring your **chin in on to your chest**, because you won't want to have a bump on the back of your head!

Falling Backwards

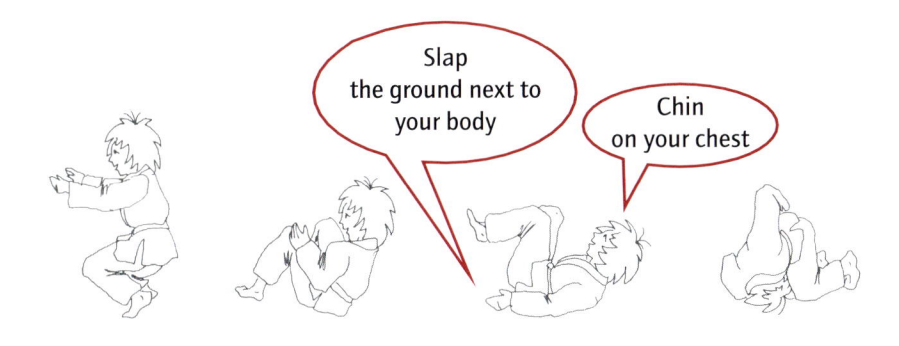

Squat down and stretch your arms out in front of your body. Now just simply roll backwards and slap the mat hard with **your arms stretched out** right next to your body. Don't forget to pull your **chin in on to your chest**. You can roll right over if you want to.

BREAKFALL TECHNIQUES 2

Falling Sideward

Standing up, **stretch the arm and the leg on the same side of the body** and keep them stretched-out during the whole movement – as if they were attached to the strings of a puppet.

With the other hand you can grab hold of your lapel, so that you don't confuse which arm you should stretch out by mistake. Now let yourself fall down as if you were slipping on a banana skin.

To do this, first of all, bend your standing leg and then drop down onto your bottom.

The 'puppet's' leg stays stretched-out and the stretched-out arm slaps the mat right next to your body, which falls down **sideways**. Don't forget to keep your chin on your chest.

BREAKFALL TECHNIQUES 3

Forward Roll

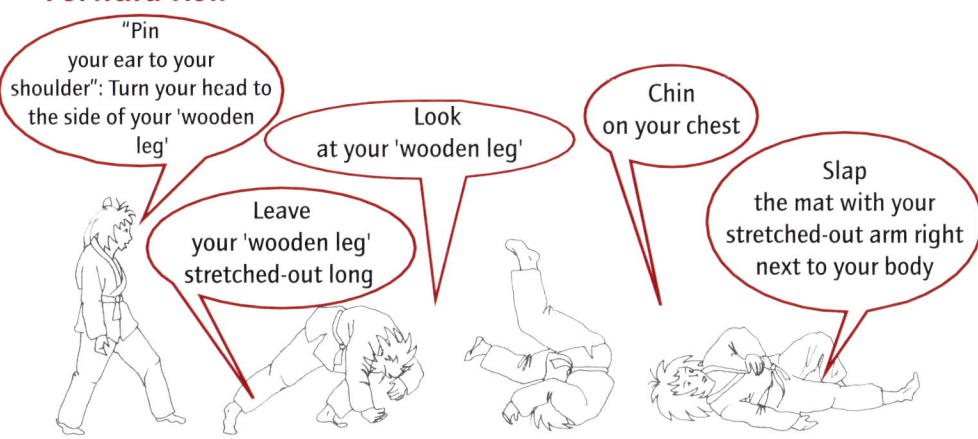

"Pin your ear to your shoulder": Turn your head to the side of your 'wooden leg'

Leave your 'wooden leg' stretched-out long

Look at your 'wooden leg'

Chin on your chest

Slap the mat with your stretched-out arm right next to your body

The forward roll must be practised both to **the right and the left,** because your partner can also throw you forward to the right and the left, according to which side he has turned to do the throw. For the forward roll to the left put your left leg forward, lay your head on to the right shoulder ('pin your ear to your shoulder'). Lift your left arm upwards with the elbow and the little finger pointing outwards. You now do a roll over this bent arm (little finger is parallel to the mat). If your arm stays nice and rounded it will protect your head and your shoulder, and you won't hurt yourself. The rear (right) leg stays stretched-out straight ('wooden leg') until you are lying sideways on the ground again. The arm on the 'wooden leg' side (right) **slaps the mat right next to your body**. Don't forget to keep your chin on your chest.

A TIP FOR THE BEGINNER:

To begin with, it's easier if you start off with your left leg forwards and then stoop down and place the back of your hand (the fingers pointing to the rear foot) on the ground - your hand and both feet form a triangle. Move your left hand to the rear between the hand on the ground and the forward leg, fingers leading. Your fingers scrape lightly over the mat's surface. And now – hey presto – you do a forward roll. Your rear leg stays stretched-out and the long arm slaps down on the same side.

BREAKFALL TECHNIQUES 4

Free breakfall

"Pin your ear to your shoulder": Head held to the side of your 'wooden leg'

Roll right forward over the arm

Leave your 'wooden leg' stretched-out long

Look at your 'wooden leg'

Chin on your chest

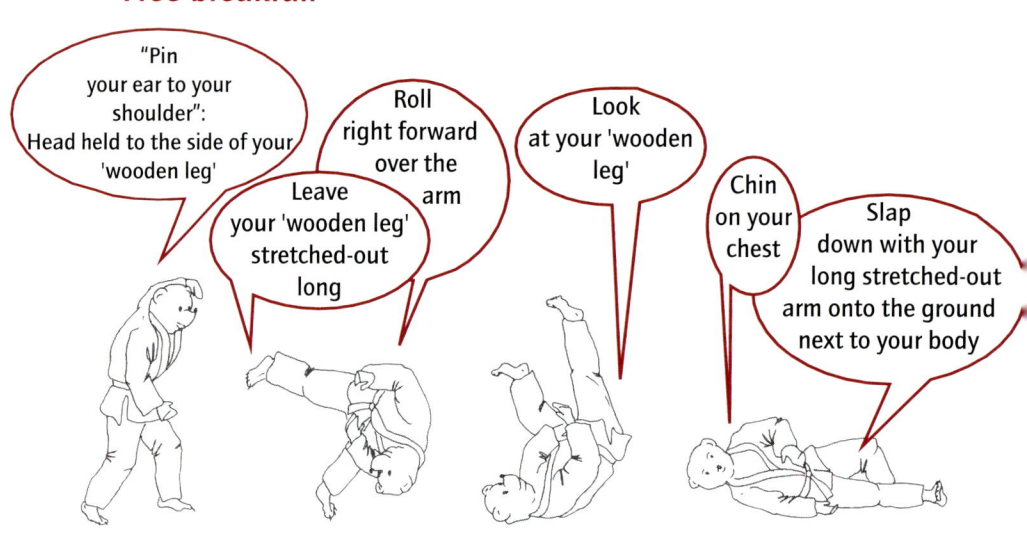

Slap down with your long stretched-out arm onto the ground next to your body

The free breakfall is an extension of the forward roll, which you can try out when you have mastered the forward roll. This time the arm creates more swing and you do a forward (flying) roll in the air, before you come to a rest lying on the side. You leave your leg stretched-out long, lift your head up high and slap the mat with your stretched-out arm right next to your body.

2 GRIPPING METHODS

KUMI-KATA

The most important thing in Judo is, first of all, to get your grip so that you can throw your opponent. This is the reason often why, in a competition, it's all about who is **first to gain the upper hand with the grip**. While it permits you to be able **to throw your partner, it also allows you to sense what his next movement will be** – and this is just as important. We show you here some of the more common gripping methods. The others you will find demonstrated in the throws later on, and you will find them particularly useful.

The sleeve and high collar grip (right-handed)

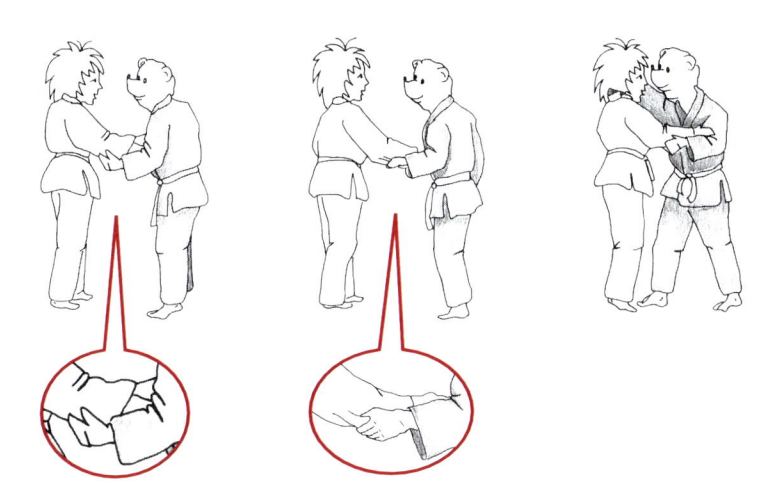

First of all, grasp the sleeve of your partner with the left hand. In doing this you grasp between his elbow and the end of his sleeve along the **seam**, which is on the underside of the sleeve on all judo clothing. Gather up as much of the material as possible into your hand and then twist your thumb into the material. **The jacket is now tensed up firmly** around the arm and gives you **good control** over your partner's movements. Now pull this arm to your body and with the other hand grasp the neck of the jacket behind the partner's head. With the *sleeve and lapel grip* (lapel grasped in front of the chest) it is just as important to have good control over the partner's arm.

KUMI-KATA

The diagonal grip over the shoulder

You adopt the right-footed stance and your partner the left-footed stance, so that you are unable to get hold of his right arm. Therefore you grasp your partner's arm with your left hand and pull it **across in front of your stomach**.

At the same time you reach **right over his back** with your right hand. You pull him in close to you so that the whole of your arm is in **contact** with his back (arm is bent and the shoulder pushed forward).

You continue to pull him in with the left hand and **additionally press down onto his shoulder with your own** so that he can't stand upright. From this position you can now execute various types of throws.

TAKE NOTE
In a competition, this one-sided gripping method must be followed very quickly by a throw.

As well as developing your own grip, it is just as important to be able to break the opponent's unwelcome grip on yourself, so that you can apply your grip. The best way to break a grip is to use **controlled and explosive** movements, which are often supported by the whole of your body. Some ways to successfully achieve this are shown here now.

3 BREAKING THE GRIP

BREAKING THE GRIP 1

Breaking the high collar grip

Your partner has succeeded in gaining a strong high collar grip (here on the right). **You reach for his shoulder from the outside and jam his arm between your head and your shoulder.** You now twist your upper body and by so doing you push your **shoulder (and hip) forwards in an explosive movement.** The movement is accentuated by moving the weight of your body forwards. You can now break your partner's grip with your arm and shoulder and then apply your own grip.

Breaking the sleeve grip

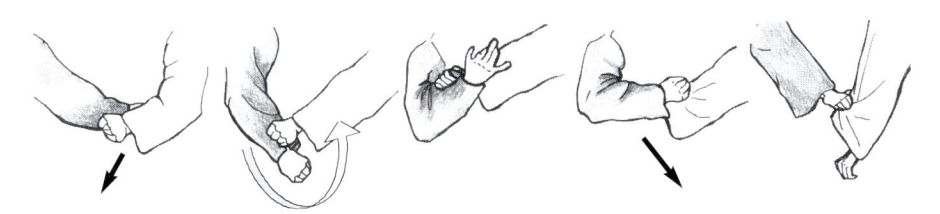

Your partner has grabbed you firmly by the arm and tries to take control of you. By pulling your arm sideways and downwards, you **pull his arm** straight and twist your hand round **from inside, downwards to the outside and then from the outside onto the sleeve of your partner and grab hold of it.** Now, you push your arm **explosively downwards** in order to break his grip. You hold his arm firmly and follow up with a throw.

BREAKING THE LAPEL GRIP 2

Breaking the lapel grip

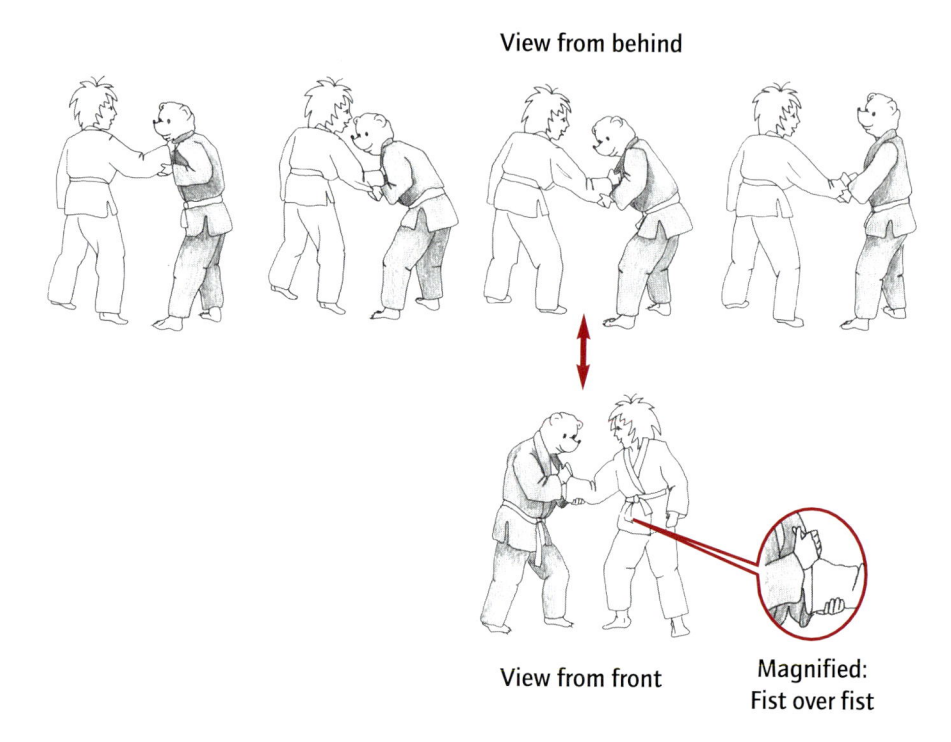

View from behind

View from front

Magnified: Fist over fist

Your partner is using a lapel grip. You grasp his sleeve on the outside by the seam so that his **jacket is wrapped firmly** round his arm. Pull downwards. With your other hand you place your fist (unclenched) over his (don't take hold of his thumb). Lean your upper body slightly forwards and bend your knees.

You now free yourself by making a **rapid upwards lift of your body** from the knees. At the same time you **push your hands away downwards** while your fists press his away from the lapel. The hand, which has grasped the arm, is pushed hard downwards. You can now follow up with a throw.

4 SEQUENCE MOVES

FOOTWORK SKILLS

Sequence moves (also called a change of stance) are a series of footwork sequences, which allow you to 'set up' the opponent in the best way for a throw. According to the situation you will need to employ different sequences. On the following pages we have laid out some of the basic sequence positions so that if you aren't sure you can refer to them later. However, it doesn't matter if you skip these pages and start off straight away with the throws. You can always leaf back and also work at the corresponding exercises when you want to.

Let's look at the footwork skill sequences first of all: There's the **parallel stance** (feet side by side), the **right stance** (right foot forward) and the **left stance** (left foot forward).

Parallel stance   **Right stance**   **Left stance**

According to the **starting situation** (your partner is pulling, pushing or something similar), you will choose the most suitable sequence for a throw – which one you choose is dependent on your partner's movements and your intended throwing method. Very often several different sequences are possible. In addition to the stances shown above, there are **mixed and transitional forms**. When you can really master the basic forms for the sequence, you will probably be able to shorten the sequence of steps in order to allow a quicker turn in, thus preventing your partner to counter your movements. These thoughts are, however, mainly for the advanced of you – even the best Judoka have started off using the basic simple sequences.

To be able to throw your partner, you have to attempt (during the sequence) to get as far as possible **under his centre of balance**. You can do this by adopting a **"elastic knees"** (knees bent slightly forward) stance. It is also possible to use a stance with **feet straddled apart** or a **normal walking stance.**

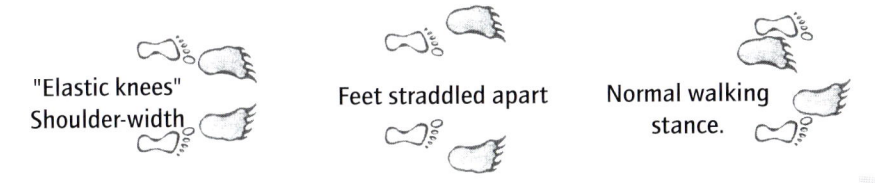

"Elastic knees" Shoulder-width   **Feet straddled apart**   **Normal walking stance.**

21

PULLING OUT SEQUENCE

The Sequence

1 2 3 4

Charlie Chaplin Steps

1 2 3

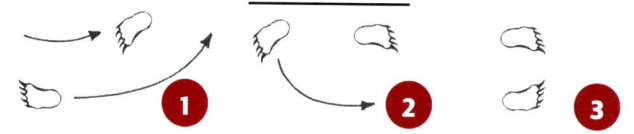

SITUATION:

Partner is pushing hard
You are moving backwards

READING NOTES:

You put your right foot to the rear and turn it inwards (so that the toes are pointing at the other heel). You turn that foot round (so that the toes are pointing in a forward direction) and bend your knees (elastic knees). You are now standing like a clown ('Charlie Chaplin Steps'). You pull the partner up ('look at your watch') in order to put him off balance. You now put your right foot round next to the left one (stay with knees bent as in Figure 3).

- Go back right and turn inwards
- Charlie Chaplin Steps
- Look at your watch
- Pull your feet together

22

KODOKAN-SEQUENCE (Rearwards)
(Kodokan is the central Dojo in Tokyo)

The Sequence

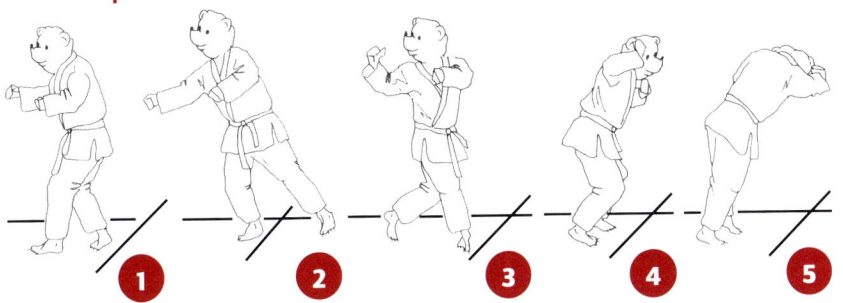

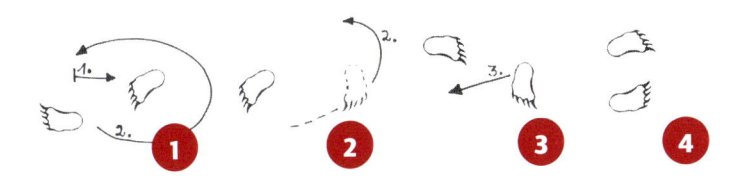

SITUATION:

Partner is pushing lightly or you are pulling
You are moving backwards

- Go back right and turn inwards
- Turn left in a backwards tight half-circle
- Look at your watch
- Right (foot) next to the left

READING NOTES:

In this sequence you glide along dropping deeper into your knees. You put your right foot to the rear and turn it inwards (so that the toes are pointing at the other heel). You place your left foot in a tight half-circle backwards and round between your partner's feet. You pull the partner up in order to put him off balance (look at your watch). You now put your right foot round next to the left one and stretch out the legs to do the throw (bend over the upper body).

TIP FOR THE ADVANCED PUPIL:

You can shorten Phase 2 and 3 into one jump.
You must tuck your bottom right into the front of the partner's thigh (i.e., get under his centre of balance).

23

KODOKAN-SEQUENCE (Forward)

The Sequence

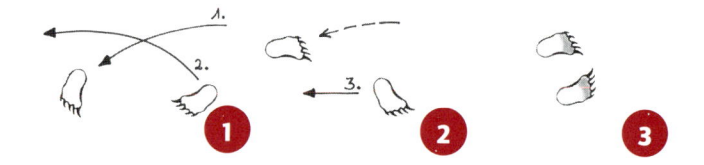

SITUATION:

Partner is pulling lightly or standing still

You are moving forwards or standing still

READING NOTES:

You put your right foot forwards in front of your partner's right foot (T-step) and begin to pull him in (look at your watch). Now you swing your left foot in a tight half-circle round between your partner's legs. As you take this step you drop down lower into your knees ('elastic knees'). Place your right foot next to your left one. You must tuck your bottom right into the front of the partner's thigh (i.e., get under his centre of balance).

- T-step to the right
- Turn left in a backwards tight half-circle
- Look at your watch
- "Elastic knees"
- Right (foot) next to the left

STRAIGHT SEQUENCE
(For a TAI OTOSHI this time)

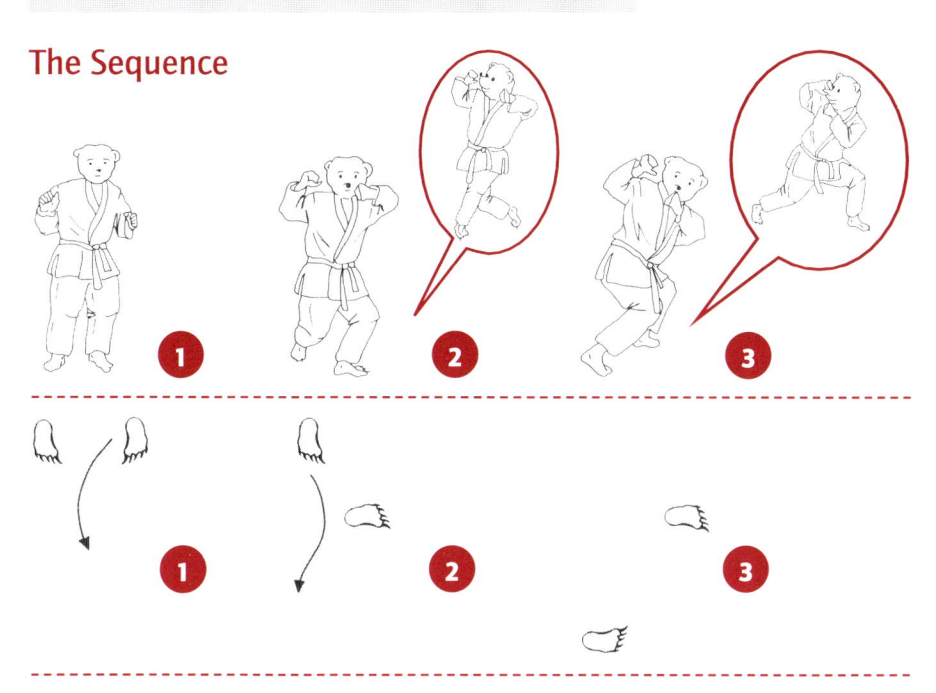

The Sequence

SITUATION:

Partner is standing still or pulling

You are moving forwards or sideways

READING NOTES:

You put your left foot forwards pushing and turning your heel to the front and at the same time bending your knees with your weight on the forward foot. Doing this you pull your partner forwards. Now you use your other leg for the throw (here, for example, for a TAI OTOSHI).

- Go left with your heels
- "Elastic knees"
- Pull down

KAWAISHI-SEQUENCE

(Mikinosuke Kawaishi was a Japanese Judo fighter, who greatly influenced European Judo)

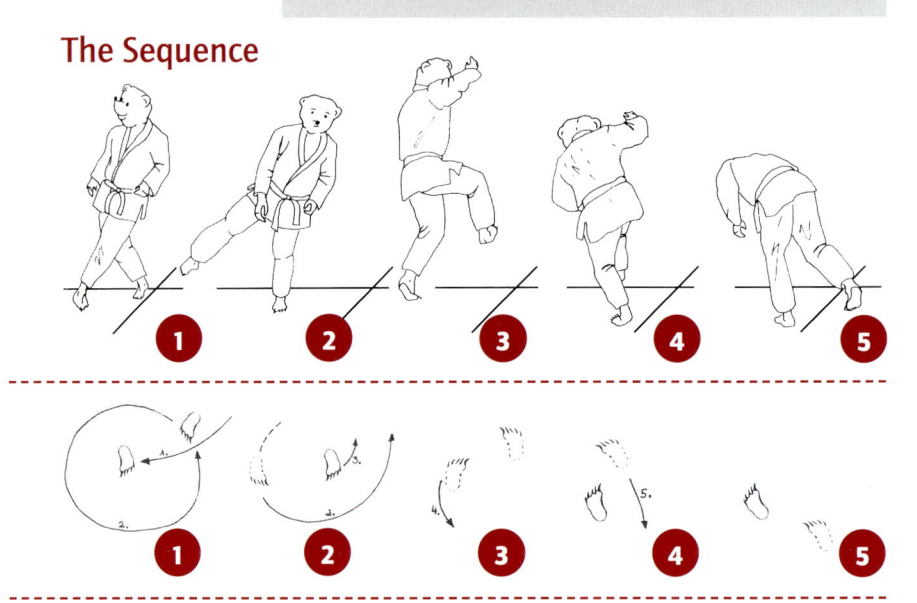

The Sequence

SITUATION:

Partner is standing still

You are moving freely

READING NOTES:

You cross your left foot sideways over the other leg with the toes pointing towards your partner in order to build up tension in the hip area (temple dancer stance). With your right foot you swing your foot in a broad circular movement, so that, with a little jump with your standing leg, you turn in close to your partner. You pull your arm forwards at the same time diagonally.

- Temple dancer stance
- Broad circular motion
- Pull forwards
- Jump at your partner

SEQUENCES - EXERCISES PART 1

(The following exercises are suggested as additional ones to the throws. You don't have to answer them straight away at the beginning.)

Exercise 1
Here are descriptions of various movements. Using a few words, describe which sequences there are for each movement. Several answers are possible.

If UKE is pushing strongly,	→	**then** I will use...
If UKE is pulling lightly,	→	**then** I will use...
If I am standing in a right footed stance,	→	**then** I will use...
If UKE is pushing lightly,	→	**then** I will use...
If I pull UKE in a circular motion,	→	**then** I will use...
If we move together in a sideways movement,	→	**then** I will use...

Exercise 2
In all the sequences, it says that you have to bend the knees like "elastic knees" - what reason can you think of for this?

_____
_____
_____

Exercise 3
A little dictionary practise: What do HAJIME, MATTE, TORI and UKE mean?

HAJIME = _____   TORI = _____
MATTE = _____   UKE = _____

28

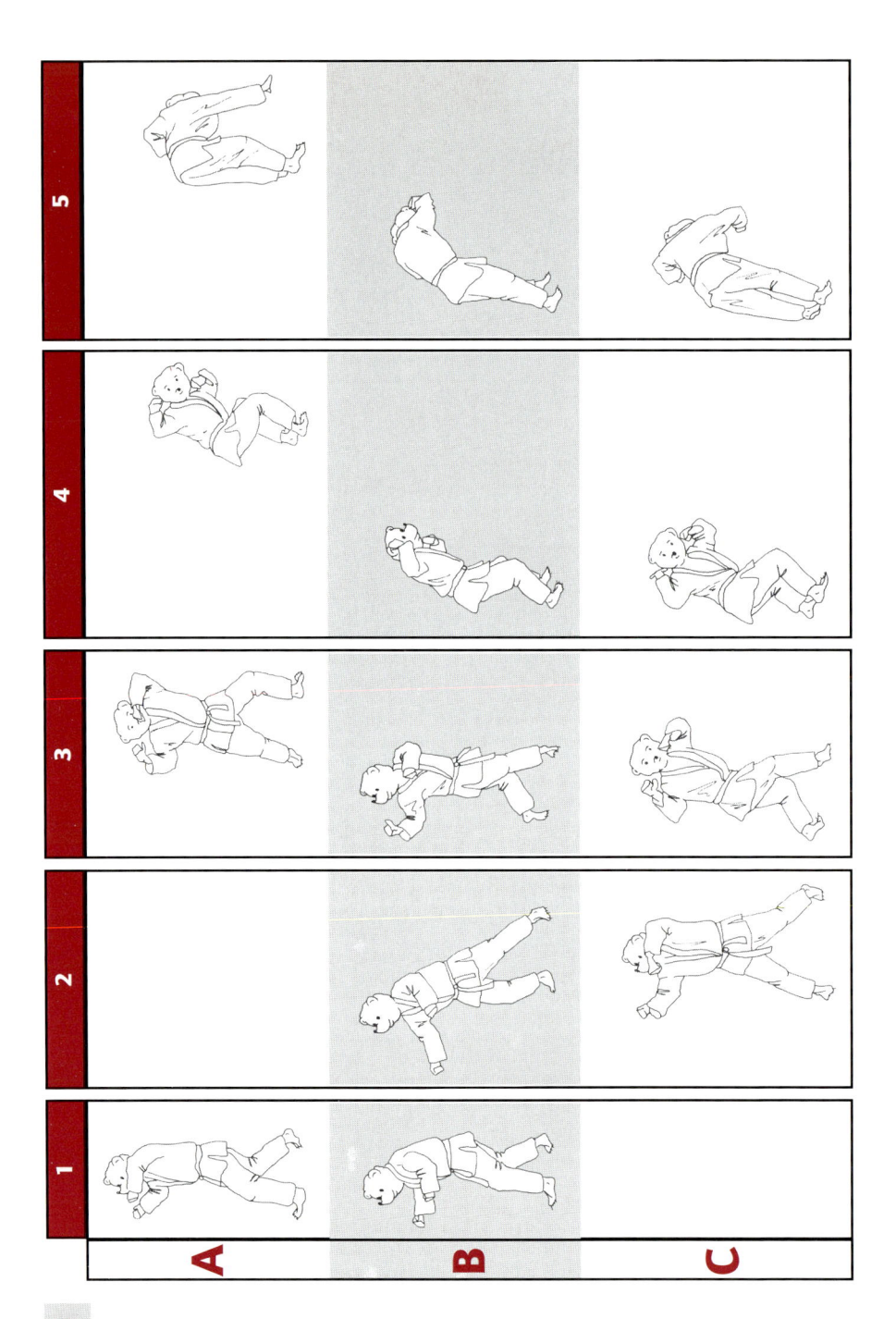

SEQUENCES – EXERCISES PART 2

Exercise 4
In the sketch on Page 28, you will see three different sequences depicted (A, B, C). Which sequences are they?

A:

B:

C:

Exercise 5
Compare Sequence **B** and **C**. What common points occur to you?

Which step is clearly different in **B** and **C** and why?

SEQUENCES – EXERCISES PART 3

Exercise 6
In what situations (UKE's and/or TORI's movements) do you use which of the sequences **A**, **B** or **C**?

A: _____

B: _____

C: _____

Exercise 7
The rearwards KODOKAN and the PULLING OUT sequences are both carried out by you from a rearwards movement. The speed of your backward movement is determined by UKE. This is the deciding factor and the reason for choosing one or the other of the sequences. When do you chose which sequence? Give the reasons why.

_____
_____
_____
_____

Exercise 8
Just imagine you want to do a KOSHI GURUMA throw. Which of the five sequences described can you use for this throw? Which factors do you use to make your decision for one or the other?

_____
_____
_____
_____

5. THROWING EXERCISES

5.1 WHITE/YELLOW BELT
O GOSHI (Major Hip Throw)

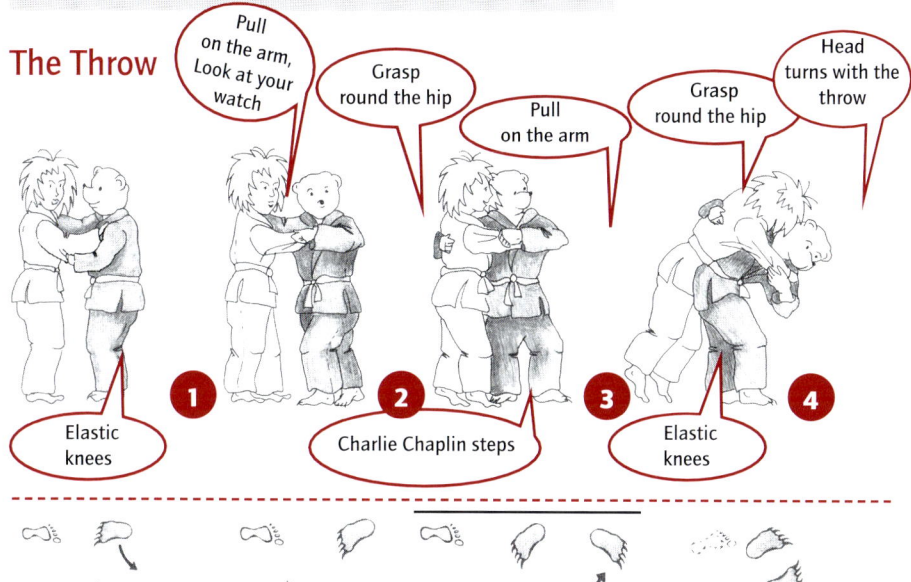

The Throw

1. Pull on the arm, Look at your watch — Elastic knees
2. Grasp round the hip / Pull on the arm — Charlie Chaplin steps
3. Grasp round the hip — Elastic knees
4. Head turns with the throw

---

1. Go back to the right and turn inwards
2. Charlie Chaplin steps
3. Forward to the right
4.

Move right to the rear, turn inwards flip in Charlie Chaplin gear, grab him by the hip, look at the watch with the eye, to get your arm right up high, elastic knees, forward right, turn, now the head turns too, and through the air right wide he flew!

READING NOTES:

Right-handed lapel grip so that your right hand grasps the partner's jacket in front of his chest. UKE is pushing. For this throw you keep an elastic knees stance. First of all place the right foot rearwards so that the big toe is pointing at the heel of the other foot. Now move your left foot to adopt a Charlie Chaplin step in line (use the edge of the mat to orient yourself). At the same time pull hard with your left arm into your body (look at your watch). Grasp your partner round the hip with your right hand. Put the right foot forward again - remember keep elastic knee stance, and throw by pulling him with a pull of your arm over your hip and back, looking over the shoulder of your pulling hand as you do (turn your head with the throw).

5.1 White/Yellow Belt

O GOSHI

Exercise 1
Colour in TORI in the four O GOSHI sketches below.

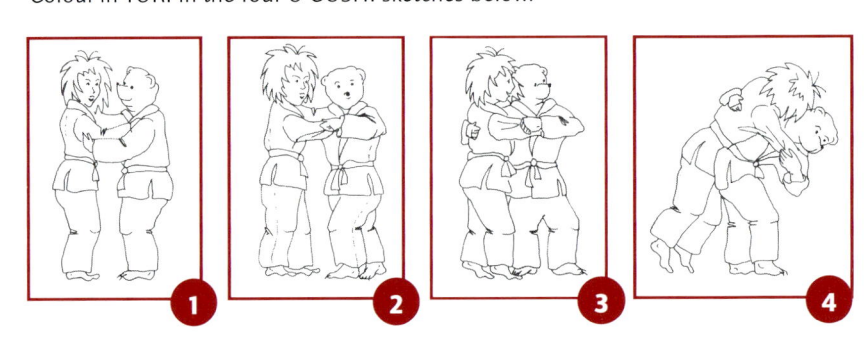

Exercise 2
The sketches show Phase 4 of the O GOSHI and also the 4th Phase of another throw. Compare the two similar pictures and circle the differences. Which picture depicts the O GOSHI – A or B? What must you watch out for in this phase of the O GOSHI throw? (Try to remember the Stardust rhyme...)

Exercise 3
Your vocabulary exercise: What do GOSHI, O, MOKUSO and REI mean?

GOSHI = _____   REI = _____
O = _____   MOKUSO = _____

5.1 White/Yellow Belt

O SOTO OTOSHI
(Major Outer Drop Throw)

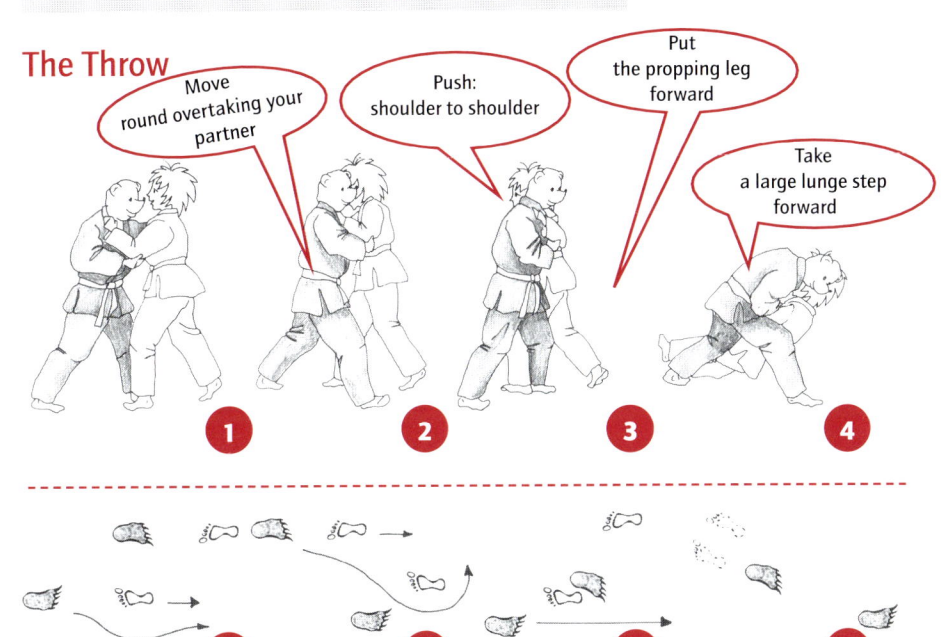

The Throw

1. Move round overtaking your partner
2. Push: shoulder to shoulder
3. Put the propping leg forward
4. Take a large lunge step forward

READING NOTES:

Overtaking along his side you go. Then prop and press. And o'er the top you throw.

You execute this throw from your own forward movement using here the left-handed hold. Of course you can also use the right-handed hold, just as you can do with all the throws explained in this section. Taking a large step forward you overtake your partner with your right foot. Your left foot props around his left leg. At the same time you push your partner off balance by moving your left shoulder forward until it is in close contact with his shoulder. You press him over until he begins to fall while you then add to this movement by taking a large lunge step with your right leg forwards. Your partner must not forget to keep his chin on his chest as he falls.

33

5.1 White/Yellow Belt

O SOTO OTOSHI

Exercise 1
Which phase of the throw is illustrated in the sketch here? What do you think is particularly important about this phase of the throw?

_____
_____
_____
_____

Exercise 2
Cut out the sketches below and stick them in the places here so that they are in the correct order for the throw.

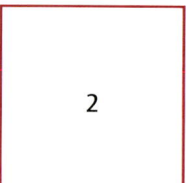

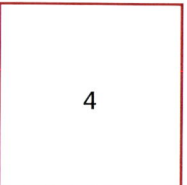

| 1 | 2 | 3 | 4 |

Exercise 3
Your vocabulary exercise: What do the following words mean?

O = _____ OTOSHI = _____
SOTO = _____ TORI = _____

5.1 White/Yellow Belt

SASAE TSURI KOMI ASHI
(Supporting Foot Lift-Pull Throw)

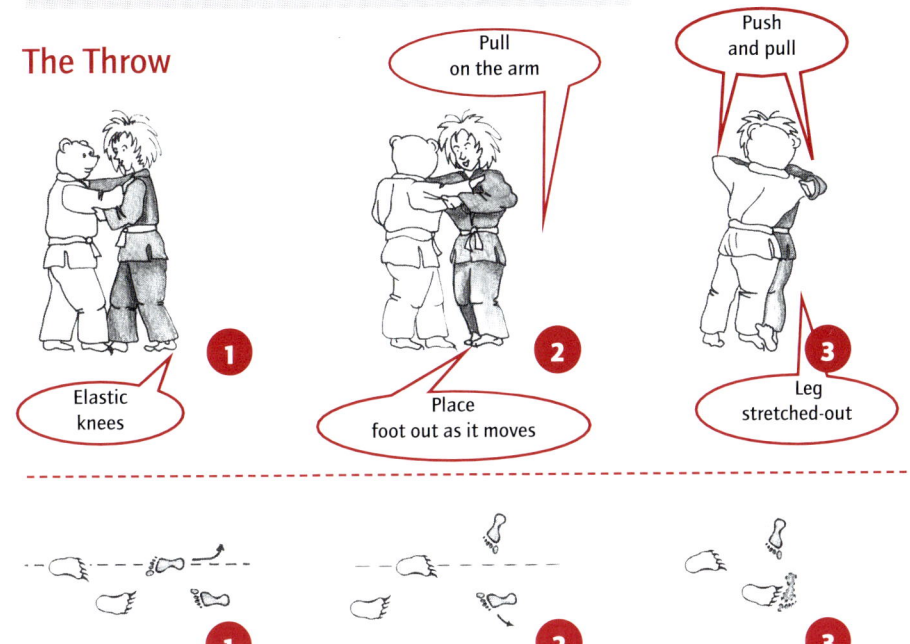

The Throw

- Pull on the arm
- Push and pull
- Elastic knees — 1
- Place foot out as it moves — 2
- Leg stretched-out — 3

Like the Torero in the ring,
it's all about the side step thing:
With outstretched leg, and strong-armed pull,
down you drag him like a bull.

READING NOTES:

For this throw you use the right-handed grip and a backwards movement whenever your partner is pushing forward. First of all place your left foot straight back. Then bring your right foot to the side. At the same time keep "elastic knees" and be ready to use a strong pull of the arm (– look at your watch). Using a strong pull of the arm and pushing with the other arm (grip out the high collar of your partner) you execute the throw over your stretched-out leg. Your partner falls down just where you were standing.

TIP FOR THE ADVANCED PUPIL:

Try using this throw against the grip, i. e. your hand at grip at the high collar pulls and the hand at grip at your partners arm is now pushing!

5.1 White/Yellow Belt

SASAE TSURI KOMI ASHI

Exercise 1
Cut out the sketches below and stick them in the places here so that they are in the correct order for the throw.

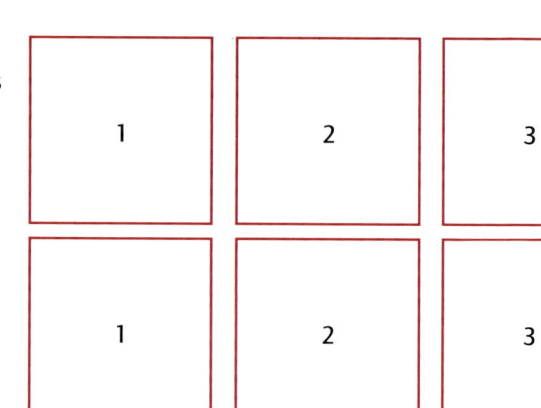

| 1 | 2 | 3 |

| 1 | 2 | 3 |

Exercise 2
What do you have watch out for when you use the SASAE TSURI KOMI ASHI? (Try to remember the Stardust formula...)

_____

_____

Exercise 3
Complete the following sentence: If UKE is pushing strongly, the throw I will use is

_____

Exercise 4
Your vocabulary exercise: What do SASAE, ASHI, and SOTO mean?

SASAE = _____
ASHI = _____
SOTO = _____

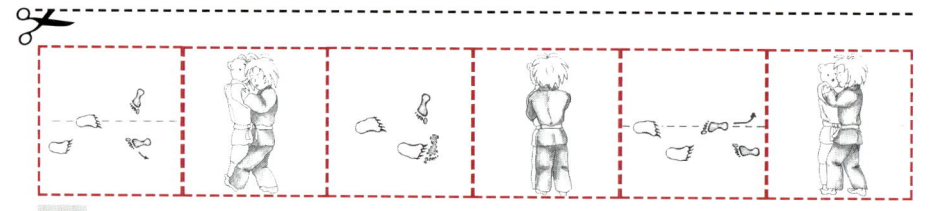

5.1 White/Yellow Belt

DE ASHI BARAI (Backwards)
(Forward foot sweep)

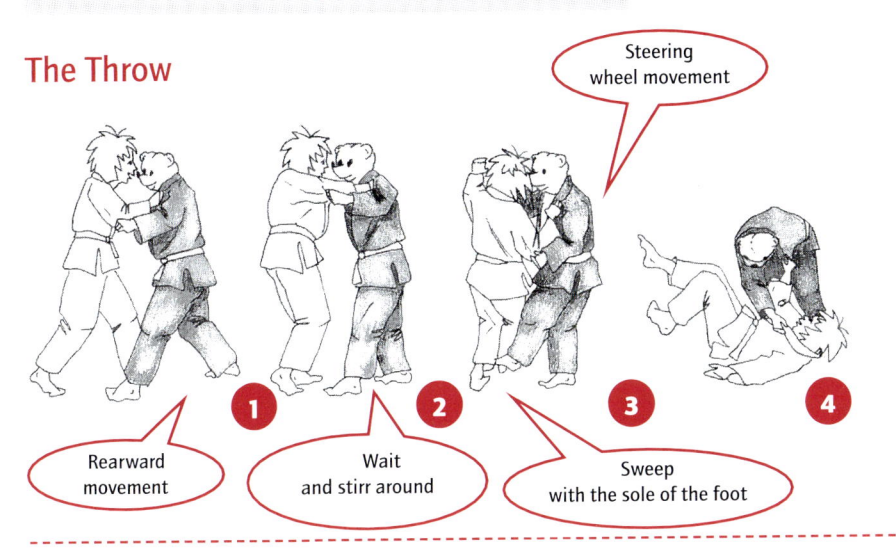

The Throw

- Steering wheel movement
- 1 Rearward movement
- 2 Wait and stir around
- 3 Sweep with the sole of the foot
- 4

Your partner's pushing, so back you go. Your lower leg stirrs round and low, long sweeping leg from hip to heel, your arms control the stirring wheel!

READING NOTES:

For this throw you use the right-handed grip and a backwards movement; your partner – here the little pixie (UKE) – is moving forwards. Now you wait until UKE's leg comes forward and then sweep through with the sole of your foot with a stirring movement before she places her foot down. When doing the sweeping movement your leg is stretched-out and your hips come forward. At the same time you pull with the arm that is holding onto your partner's sleeve, twisting downwards and to the inside, while at the same time you move your other arm in the opposite direction (steering wheel movement).

5.1 White/Yellow Belt

DE ASHI BARAI (Backwards)

Exercise 1
Cut out the sketches below and stick them in the places here so that they are in the correct order for the throw.

1	2	3
1	2	3

Exercise 2
What do you have watch out for when you use the DE ASHI BARAI? (Try to remember the Stardust formula...)

_____
_____
_____

Exercise 3
Your vocabulary exercise: What do ASHI, BARAI and GOSHI mean?

ASHI = _____
BARAI = _____
GOSHI = _____

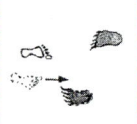

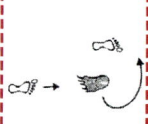

38

5.1 White/Yellow Belt

DE ASHI BARAI (Forwards)
(Forward Foot Sweep)

The Throw

1 Forward movement

2 Starting step

3 Sweep round with the sole of the foot — Steering wheel movement

4

Uke steps back, so you step fore, your leg is sweeping one time more, be sure to drive your stirring wheel, then he will fall, that´s no big deal!

READING NOTES:

For this throw you use the right-handed grip and a forward movement; your partner – here the little bear (UKE) – is moving backwards.

When the little bear has got the weight of his body over the rear standing leg, you (the little pixie) sweep his unweighted leg with the sole of your foot.

When doing the sweeping movement your leg is stretchedout and your hips come forward. At the same time you pull with the arm that is holding onto your partner's sleeve, twisting downwards and to the inside (stirring wheel movement).

5.1 White/Yellow Belt

DE ASHI BARAI (Forwards)

Exercise 1
Cut out the sketches below and stick them in the places here so that they are in the correct order for the throw.

1	2	3

1	2	3

Exercise 2
From what you know already, how do you differentiate between the DE ASHI BARAI when moving forwards and the DE ASHI BARAI when moving backwards? (Try to remember the Stardust formula...)

_____
_____
_____

Exercise 3
Your vocabulary exercise: What do ASHI, BARAI and UKE mean?

ASHI = _____
BARAI = _____
UKE = _____

40

5.1 White/Yellow Belt

A JUDO-SAFARI STORY

Have you ever been in a safari park? That's a zoo, where the animals are not behind bars, but where people drive in their cars through large open-air enclosures with the animals running around freely. One feels sometimes really small – think of it, when an elephant sits on the car's bonnet, the bear sticks it's head through the car window and begs an apple or even an ape sits down comfortably by the windscreen and tries to bend the windscreen wipers. But we can do Judo. Judo? YES – but how? Our opponent isn't wearing Judo clothes, and we can't grasp him by the lapels. We could ask him to put on a Judo outfit – but we would have difficulties in making ourselves understood. Perhaps an O SOTO OTOSHI with a follow up grip? But then perhaps the idea isn't a good one, because if the ape manages to grab us and those long teeth.....brrr! Or, then there's perhaps our particular favourite O GOSHI throw that helped us so much in the randori recently. But, what happens when the fellow sticks to our back or lands on all fours? I suppose it's better to just stay sitting in the car and loudly state that, despite the fact that we could bring everything under control with a Judo hold, our love for animals won't allow it. The grins on the faces of our fellow passengers we will just have to ignore.

Many animals have special capabilities that we will never be able to possess, despite thorough practice; there's the speed of the kangaroo, the slyness of the fox, the slipperiness of the snake, the keen eye of the eagle, the strength of the bear and the vigour of the panther. Have you ever seen any of the animals we've mentioned moving? Well of course you may have, and you may have admired and imitated their skills. How do you get more skilled? Simply by training body and mind, keeping fit and taking part in the activities and judo programmes of your local club – ask your trainer about what you can do. A little running, jumping, throwing and other activities such as drawing, writing or modelling will train your skills. Still, your local Judo competition will all serve to remind you how much better animals can do things, where we have to put so much into it with the training...

Do you know of other animals that have capabilities that we could well use in Judo? Write them down here:

5.2 Yellow Belt

O GOSHI (Circular Movement) (Major Hip Throw)

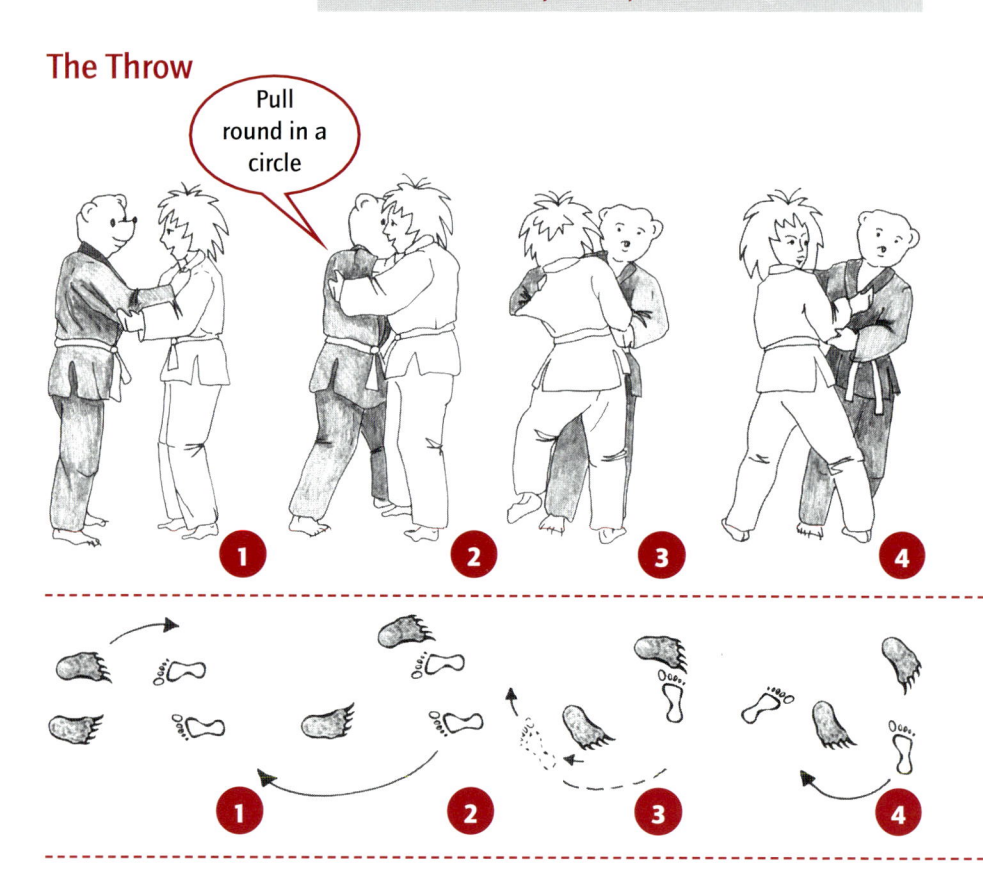

The Throw

Pull round in a circle

1 2 3 4

1 2 3 4

Pull him tumbling round and round, then stop him with your arm quite sound and solid round his hip. Now check your watch and start his trip right on time down to the ground!

READING NOTES:

This throw is carried out using a circular movement and a lapel grip. Place your left foot to the side in front of your partner and pull him round strongly in a circle with the arm gripping his lapel. He will be forced to follow round after you. You halt this circular movement by allowing him to run into your arm, which is grasping him round the waist.

5.2 Yellow Belt

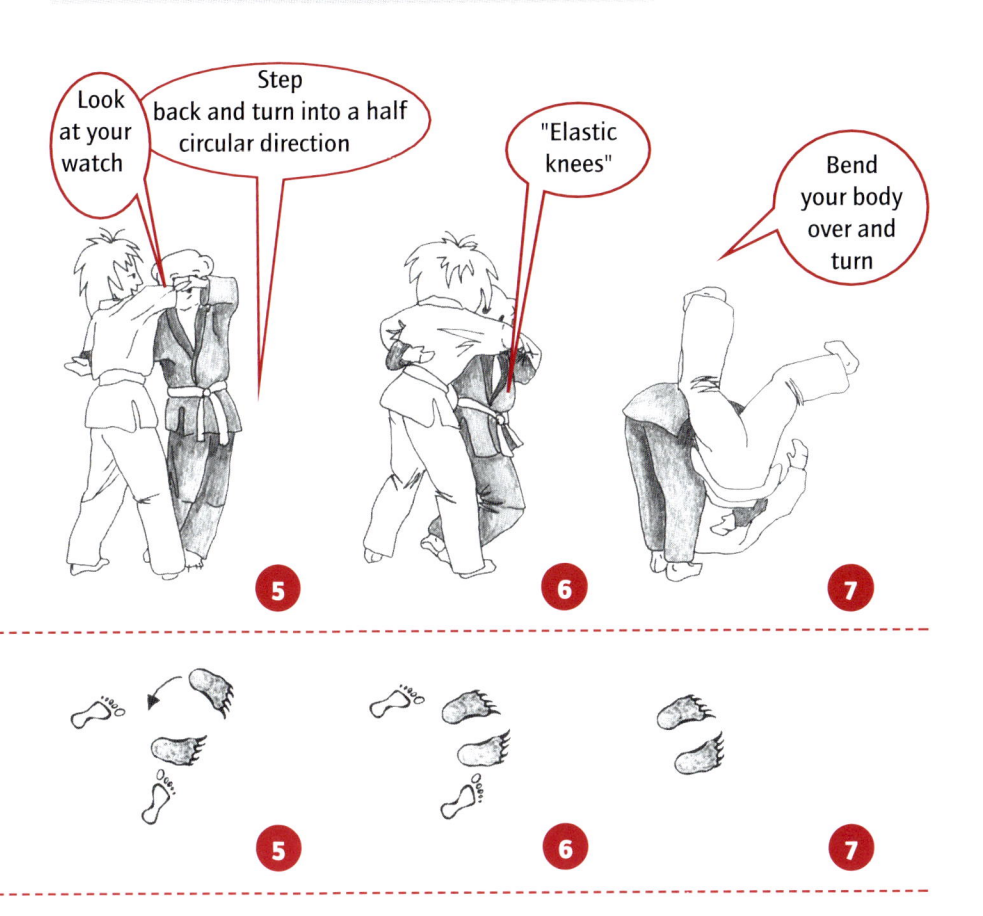

You rip his arm up with your left hand (look at your watch), while at the same time you take a step backwards in a half circular direction. Now you bend your knees (elastic knees) down low and throw him with a strong pull of your arm, at the same time bending over and turning your body.

5.2 Yellow Belt

O GOSHI (Major Hip Throw)

Exercise 1
Cut out the feet below and stick them in the places here so that they are in the correct order for the circular movement.

| 1 | 2 | 3 | 4 |

| 5 | 6 | 7 |

Exercise 2
Cut out the feet below and stick them in the places here so that they are in the correct order for the backwards movement.

| 1 | 2 | 3 | 4 |

Exercise 3
Your vocabulary exercise: What do the following words mean?

GOSHI = _____   O = _____
SOTO = _____   GURUMA = _____

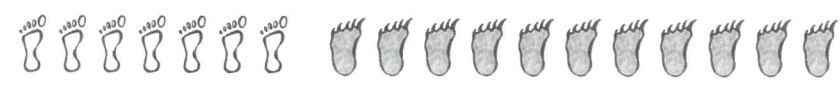

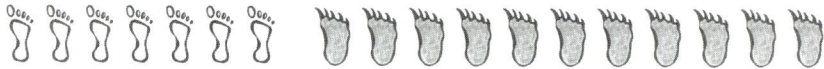

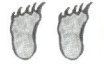

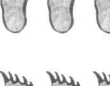

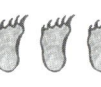

5.2 Yellow Belt

KOSHI GURUMA (Hip Wheel)

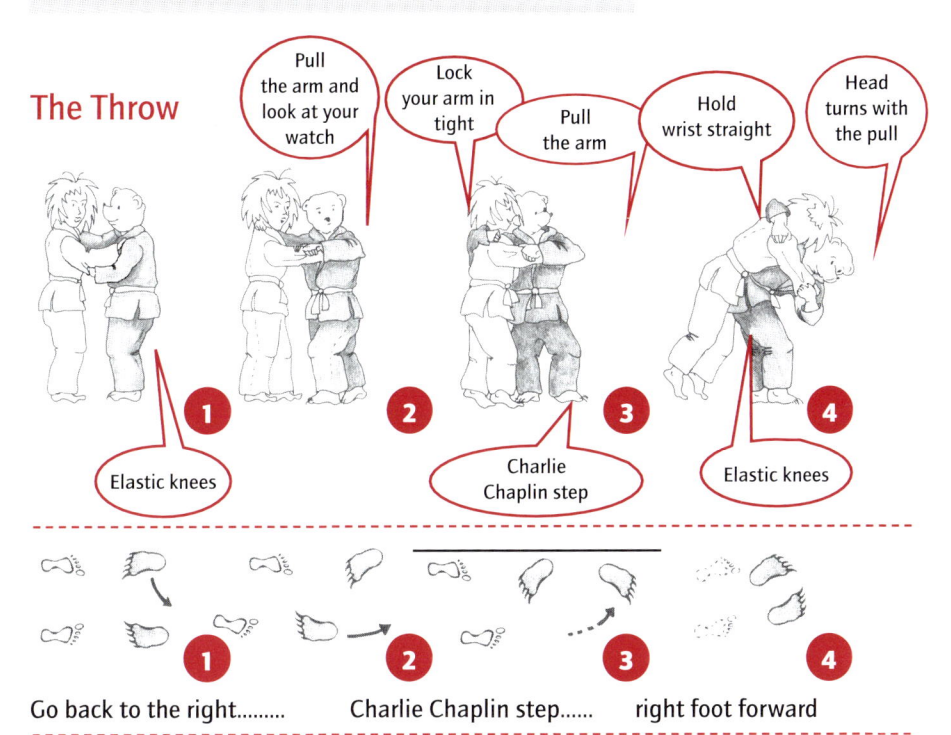

The Throw

1. Elastic knees — Pull the arm and look at your watch
2. Lock your arm in tight — Pull the arm
3. Charlie Chaplin step — Hold wrist straight
4. Elastic knees — Head turns with the pull

1. Go back to the right………
2. Charlie Chaplin step……
3. right foot forward
4.

Right foot back and turn inside, just like Charlie Chaplin slide, trap the head nice and tight. At your watch face you must gaze. It's the only way your arm to raise. Bend knees down deep, head turning keep, and your partner will change place!

READING NOTES:

Use a right-handed grip so that the right hand reaches behind the head and grabs hold of the jacket. Always stay with your knees slightly bent (elastic knees) when doing this throw. First of all you place your right foot backwards so that your big toe is pointing at the heel of the other foot. Now you move your left foot in a Charlie Chaplin fashion along a line (use the edge of the mat to guide the movement). At the same time bring your partner towards you with a strong arm pull – don't forget to look at your watch! Trap your partner hard in with your right hand. You only have to move your right foot forward, remember elastic knees, and you throw him by pulling him with a wrench of your arm over your hip, looking over the shoulder of the pulling arm as you do this. (Move your head with the throw).

5.2 Yellow Belt

KOSHI GURUMA (Hip Wheel)

Exercise 1
Draw the footprints for the PULLING-OUT sequence in the four boxes below – indicate which is UKE and TORI.

| 1 | 2 | 3 | 4 |

Exercise 2
You can see puzzle parts for the 3rd and 4th phase of the throw. Cut them out and assemble them in the two empty boxes below. What do you have to watch out for in these two phases of the throw – think of the Stardust formula...)

3

4

5.2 Yellow Belt

Exercise 3
Your vocabulary exercise: What do KOSHI, UCHI and GURUMA mean?

KOSHI   = _____   Nickname:
UCHI   = _____   _____
GURUMA   = _____   _____

What do we call the KOSHI GURUMA in English?

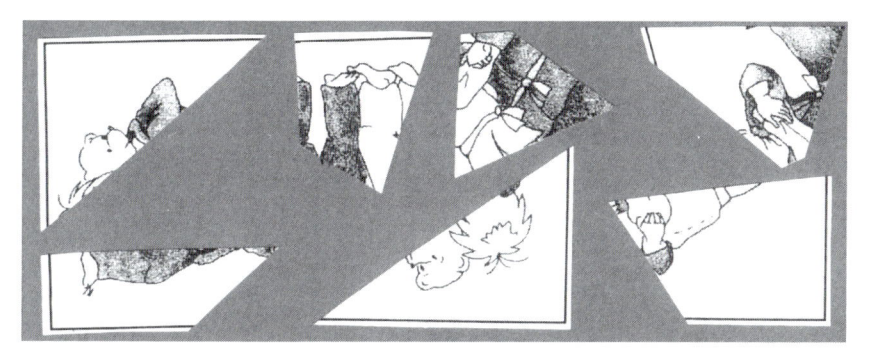

✂--

5.2 Yellow Belt

SEOI OTOSHI (Shoulder Drop)

The Throw

1. Go right to the rear and turn inwards
2. Pull the arm and look at your watch / Turn round in a circle backwards to the left
3. Lock his arms tightly / "Wrap" your leg around your partner
4. Upper body turns

Right foot back, and turn around, in a tight circle off you go. Snap and trap your partner sound. Your leg wraps round and traps him low, now pull right hard and stretch your leg, down he goes like a skittle peg.

READING NOTES:

Use a left-handed grip with a backwards movement for this throw. You step backwards and turn the right foot round so that your big toe is pointing at the heel of the other foot. Step back now with the other foot in a tight circle rearwards (KODOKAN sequence). At the same time pull your partner forwards by pulling on his lapel – don't forget to look at your watch! Using the other arm trap your partner's upper arm in the crook of your elbows (locked arms). On the same side in a wide step place your foot with a bent leg closely at your partner's leg. To execute the throw, you must use a strong pull of the arm, turn your upper body (look at your watch!) bend over and stretch your bent leg out.

48

5.2 Yellow Belt

Exercise 1
Draw the sequence of foot movements for the SEOI OTOSHI in the four boxes below – indicate which is UKE and TORI. When does TORI only step on the balls of his feet?

| 1 | 2 | 3 | 4 |

Exercise 2
Here you see two extracts from the 2nd and 3rd phase of the throw. Which important details do they show? What do you have to watch out for in these phases of the throw – think of the Stardust formula...)

Exercise 3
Your vocabulary exercise: What do SEOI, GOSHI and OTOSHI mean?

SEOI   = _____   English name:
GOSHI   = _____   _____
OTOSHI = _____   _____

What do we call the SEOI OTOSHI in English?

5.2 Yellow Belt

KO UCHI GARI (Minor Inner Reaping)

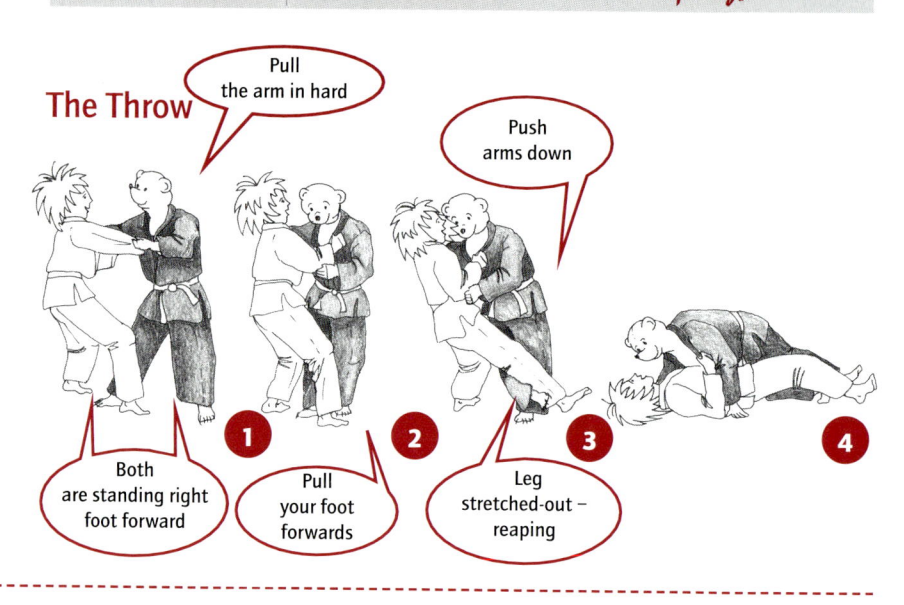

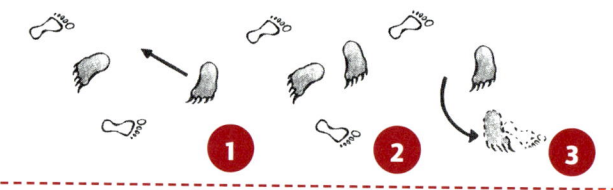

The Throw

1. Both are standing right foot forward — Pull the arm in hard
2. Pull your foot forwards
3. Leg stretched-out – reaping — Push arms down
4.

READING NOTES:

Your partner grab and hard you pull, and bring your back leg around. Stretched-out you reap with the sole to cull, and press him down into the ground.

Use a right-handed grip. You stand with your right foot a little forward, and pull your partner hard into your body. When he reacts and tries to pull away, you bring your rear foot forward and adopt a bent knee posture (elastic knees). Your forward leg now traces a reaping movement with the sole of the foot against your partner's forward leg, and reaps it away. At the same time you press his arms downwards.

Don't forget to give him a big smile as you adopt your grip!

5.2 Yellow Belt

KO UCHI GARI (Minor Inner Reaping)

Exercise 1
Briefly describe how your partner will (or will not) react when you pull him and what you then have to do. Follow the arrows.

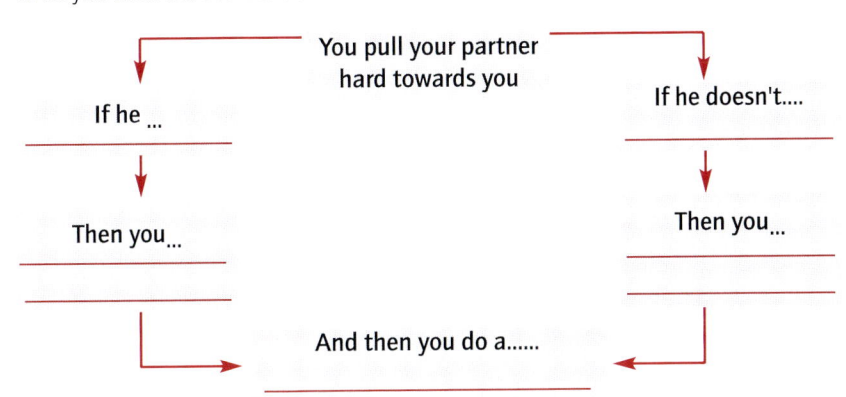

You pull your partner hard towards you

If he ...
_____

Then you...
_____
_____

If he doesn't....
_____

Then you...
_____
_____

And then you do a......
_____

Exercise 2
In the pictures here you see two individual details from the KO UCHI GARI. Which phases of the throw do the pictures belong to? Which important details do they show? What do you have to particularly watch out for in these two phases of the throw – think of the Stardust formula...)

_____
_____
_____
_____
_____
_____
_____

Exercise 3
Your vocabulary exercise: What do KO, O, SOTO, UCHI and GARI mean?

O   = _____   KO   = _____
UCHI   = _____   SOTO = _____
GARI   = _____

5.2 Yellow Belt

O UCHI GARI (Major Inner Reaping)

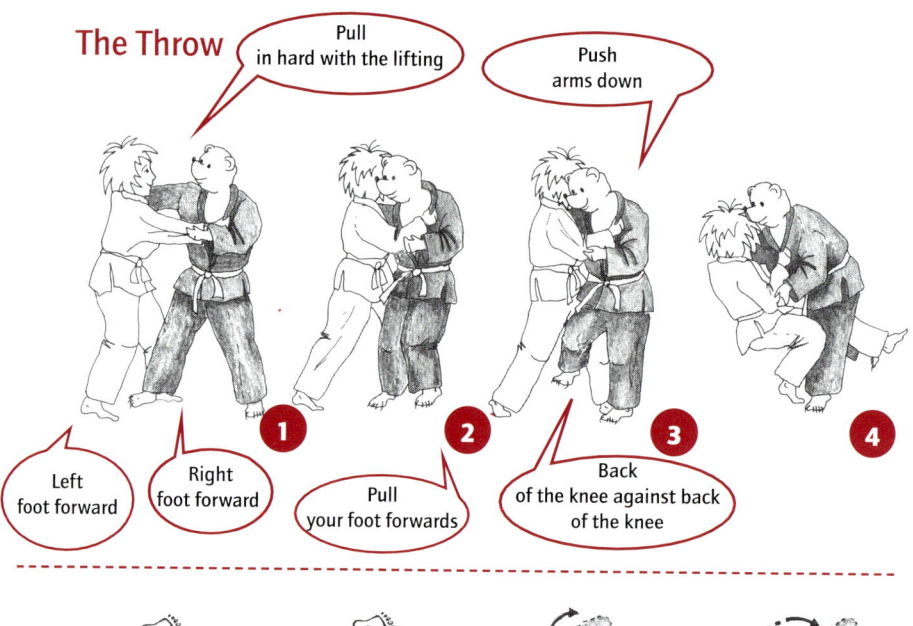

The Throw

- Pull in hard with the lifting
- Push arms down

1. Left foot forward / Right foot forward
2. Pull your foot forwards
3. Back of the knee against back of the knee
4.

You pull hard and he strinks back, step up with your posterior leg, now reap his front leg right away push down and to the ground he´ll sway!

READING NOTES:

Use a right-handed grip. You stand with your right foot forward and your partner with his left foot forward. When your partner reacts to your strong pull in and moves backwards, you pull your rear foot forward.

You now reap his front standing leg away as you execute a semi-circular movement with your forward leg. (The back of your knee locked to the back of his knee).

At the same time you press your arms downward in the direction of your reaping leg.

5.2 Yellow Belt

O UCHI GARI (Major Inner Reaping)

Exercise 1
Briefly describe how your partner will (or will not) react when you pull him and what you then have to do. Follow the arrows.

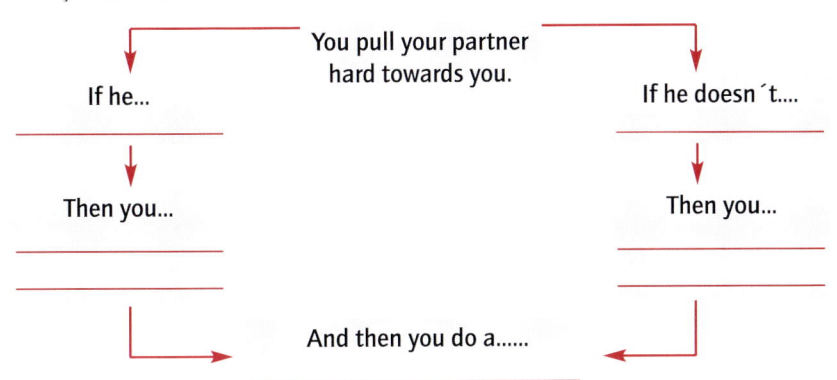

```
                 You pull your partner
                   hard towards you.
   If he...                                    If he doesn´t....
   _____                                   _____

   Then you...                                 Then you...
   _____                                   _____
   _____                                   _____

                 And then you do a......
                 _____
```

Exercise 2
In the pictures here you see the phases of the KO UCHI GARI and the O UCHI GARI. Which pictures belong to which throw? For which starting situation do you use the O UCHI GARI and why?

_____
_____
_____
_____
_____

Exercise 3
Your vocabulary exercise: What do KO, O, UCHI and GURUMA mean?

O   = _____   KO   = _____
UCHI   = _____   GURUMA = _____

53

5.2 Yellow Belt

WINNING BY GIVING IN

Once upon a time there lived a little boy called Wun, far away from here in Asia. He lived just like you and many other children do – he went to school, he tussled with other children and also played with them, and sometimes he played pranks.

Life could have been wonderful for him, if – well – if he hadn't been so small. He was always the smallest and the lightest and always came out the worst in fighting games at the monastery school and in scraps with others. He had tried everything – he ate double portions of rice and vegetables at lunch and in the evening he tried all possible kinds of exercises – but nothing helped.

One day on the way home from school he ran into a storm – a typhoon, like it often happens in Asia. Ripped off branches from trees whipped through the air all around him.

Trembling he hid in order not to be knocked down by the wind. Crouching wide-eyed in his hideout he noticed how big trees were being uprooted by the buffeting power of the wind and simply fell down. But, amongst the big uprooted trees he saw a young sapling tree that got pressed down smoothly along the ground under the wind and then supply righted itself up again as the wind fell. As soon as he could he scrambled home from the storm to his parent's hut.

The next morning the sun shone brightly in the sky. On his way to school, nothing reminded Wun any more of the storm other than the many splintered and broken trees lying around. He also saw the little sapling again. It looked a little windswept and tattered but otherwise it stood healthy and straight amongst the surrounding devastation, as if the previous day's storm had never happened.

Wun thought about the little tree as he was taking part in fighting sports at school again. Just as always, little Wun came up against a much stronger and larger opponent, but this time he didn't struggle in vain against the other's strength.

As his laughing opponent tried to press him down to the ground – he simply gave in. The larger opponent stumbled, lost his balance and fell over. Little Wun had won his first fight.

5.2 Yellow Belt

This is an old story about the beginning of Judo (JU in Japanese = gentle submission and DO = way) – the "gentle way" to success.

Think about this and consider which WAYS (techniques) you could use in Wun's place. You have now learned several throws – which one would you use when your opponent is pushing you hard? Can you do the left-handed version of it?

5.3 Yellow/Orange Belt

IPPON SEOI NAGE
(One Arm Shoulder Throw)

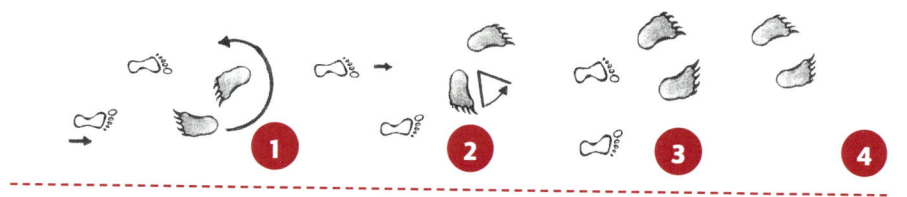

The Throw

1. Turn inwards
2. Pull the arm and look at your watch / Drop down low
3. Lock his arm
4. Bend the upper body over and turn / Stretch the legs

READING NOTES:

Right foot back, and turn inside. Then go lower in your stride. Keep your pull up nice and high, with arm lock now must not go by. Now bend right forward 'til he hovers, and onto the mat with n'ere a bother.

Use a left-handed grip. You step backwards with your right foot, at the same time turning your foot inwards. Pull your partner hard in by the lapel (look at your watch and pull up high). Simultaneously step back with the left foot in a semi-circle rearwards and drop down low in the knees until your bottom touches your partner's thigh. That way you glide right under his centre of balance. You clamp your partner's upper arm in the hollow of your elbow (lock his arm).

Don't forget to pull forward continuously.
You complete the throw by bending over your upper body and stretching your legs.

5.3 Yellow/Orange Belt

IPPON SEOI NAGE
(One Arm Shoulder Throw)

Exercise 1
Describe briefly which movements are illustrated as TORI goes through the curve in the diagram.

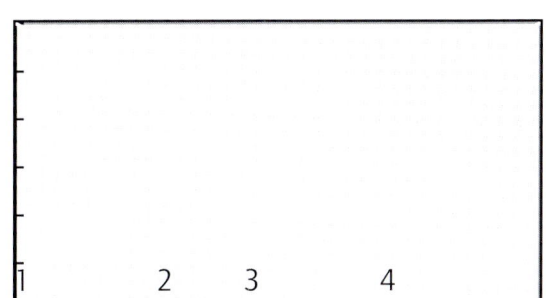

_____
_____
_____
_____

Exercise 2
Which throws are illustrated in Pictures 1 and 2? Briefly describe the details that are similar and then those, which are different.

_____
_____
_____

Exercise 3
Your vocabulary exercise: What do NAGE, GARI, OTOSHI and SEOI mean?

NAGE = _____   GARI = _____
SEOI = _____   OTOSHI = _____

Exercise 4
Which phase of the IPPON SEOI NAGE does this puzzle make?

57

5.3 Yellow/Orange Belt

TSURI KOMI GOSHI
(Lift pull Hip Throw)

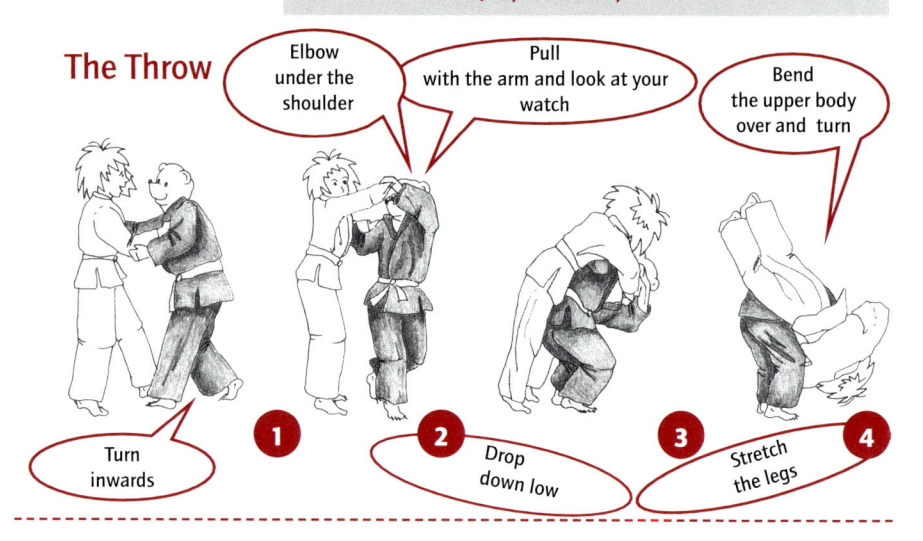

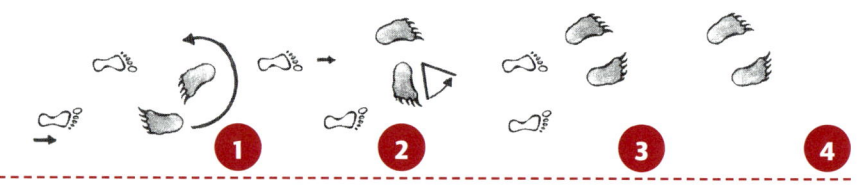

The Throw

- Elbow under the shoulder
- Pull with the arm and look at your watch
- Bend the upper body over and turn

1. Turn inwards
2. Drop down low
3. Stretch the legs
4.

READING NOTES:

Go 'long down low in your knees, and prepare your arm to pull up high. Lapel grip lift your partner please, elbow lock under shoulder apply. Now bend right forward 'til he flies, and here on the mat he finally lies.

Use a right-handed grip (of the lapel). You step backwards with your right foot and turn it inwards. When you pull round the other foot in a semi-circle and slide down low into your knees, you pull your partner's arm in an arc to the outside (look at your watch!).

With your lapel hand you pull your partner towards you and lift him by tucking your elbow under your partner's shoulder (Note: Keep a firm wrist) until your bottom touches your partner's thigh. That way you are able to glide right under your partner's centre of balance. You complete the throw by bending over your upper body and stretching and at the same time you push your elbow further under the shoulder, pulling with the other hand.

5.3 Yellow/Orange Belt

TSURI KOMI GOSHI
(Lift Pull Hip Throw)

Exercise 1
Which phase of the throw do you recognise in this illustration? Describe briefly what you can see.
_____
_____
_____
_____

Exercise 2
You use a TSURI KOMI GOSHI throw. Describe how you use your right and left hands in the throw.
_____
_____
_____
_____
_____
_____

Exercise 3
Which throws are illustrated in Pictures 1 and 2? Briefly describe the details that are similar and then those, which are different.
_____
_____
_____
_____

Exercise 4
Your vocabulary exercise: What do IPPON, TSURI, GOSHI and UKE mean?

IPPON = _____   TSURI = _____
GOSHI = _____   UKE   = _____

5.3 Yellow/Orange Belt

TAI OTOSHI (Body Drop)

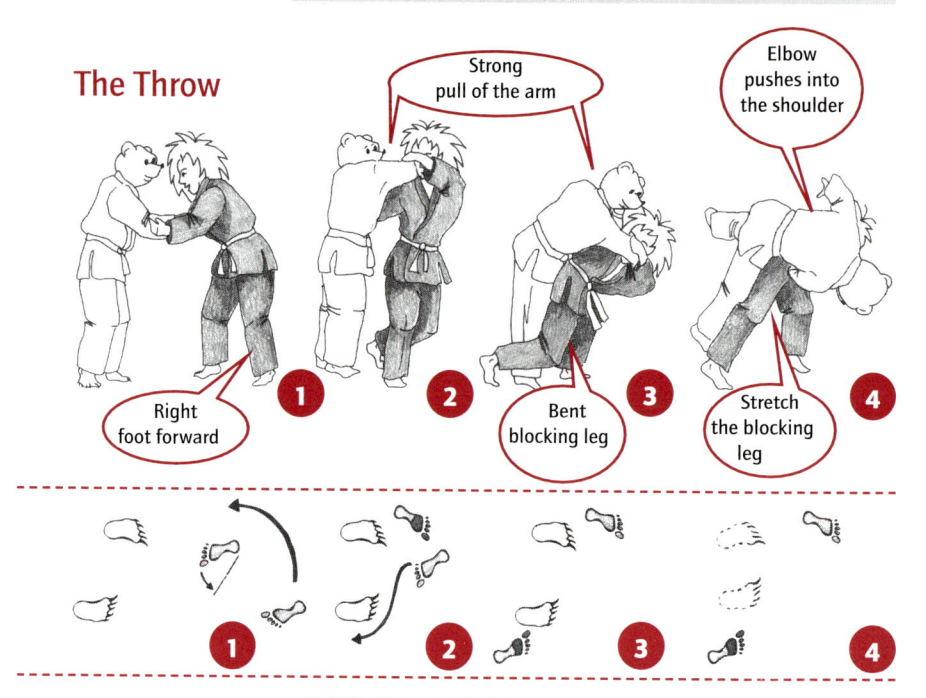

The Throw

1. Right foot forward
2. Strong pull of the arm
3. Bent blocking leg — Elbow pushes into the shoulder
4. Stretch the blocking leg

Take Care:
In order to avoid an undesirable lock of the leg, your knee must be well below UKE's knee.

> Pull in an arm and cross your feet, pushing with your own elbow neat, blocking leg close to him and bent. That's where your weight is always sent.

READING NOTES:

Stand in a right stance or a rearwards movement with right-handed hold (starting the KODOKAN reawards sequence). With a strong arching pull of the arm you bring your partner towards you (look at your watch!). At the same time swing round your rear leg in a tight semicircle (cross over at the rear). Your opposite hand pulls your partner and lifts him as your elbow presses up under his shoulder. Keeping a strong pull, you bring your bent blocking leg close alongside your partner's leg as far to the rear as possible. The knee is pointing downwards and you place only the ball of your foot down. (Take care not to let your upper body tip to one side, so that later on you are still able to put your weight on your blocking leg). You can now throw him by pushing the elbow of your opposite hand into your partner's shoulder, pulling at the same time with the other hand and finally stretching out your blocking leg.

5.3 Yellow/Orange Belt

TAI OTOSHI (Body Drop)

Exercise 1
Which throw do you recognise in this illustration? Describe briefly what you can see. What similarity with the TAI OTOSHI has the movement illustrated here?

_____
_____
_____
_____

Exercise 2
Which throws are illustrated in Pictures 1 and 2? Briefly describe the details that are similar and then those, which are different.

_____
_____
_____

Exercise 3
Which throws are illustrated in Pictures 1 and 2? Briefly describe the details that are similar and then those, which are different.

_____
_____
_____
_____

Exercise 4
Your vocabulary exercise: What do TAI, SEOI, OTOSHI and GURUMA mean?

TAI   = _____   SEOI   = _____
GURUMA = _____   OTOSHI = _____

5.3 Yellow/Orange Belt

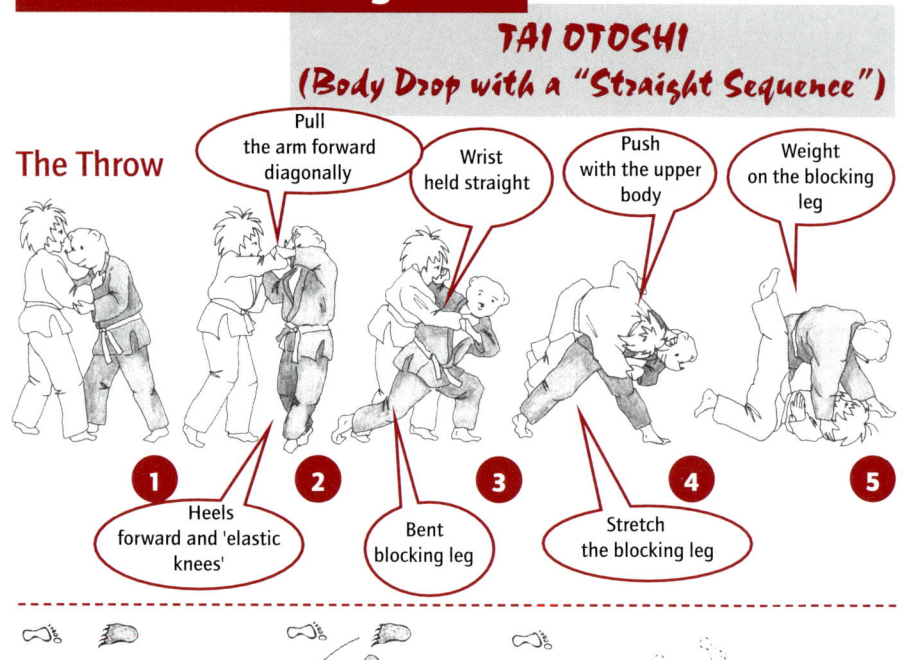

TAI OTOSHI
(Body Drop with a "Straight Sequence")

The Throw

1. Pull the arm forward diagonally
2. Wrist held straight
3. Push with the upper body
4. Weight on the blocking leg

1. Heels forward and 'elastic knees'
2.
3. Bent blocking leg
4. Stretch the blocking leg
5.

Cross your feet over to the front. Pushing with your own elbow prompt, blocking leg close to him and bent. That's where your weight is always sent.

READING NOTES:

Right foot forward and a right-handed grip. When UKE takes a step backwards, then you make a strong arching pull of the arm to bring your partner towards you (look at your watch!). At the same time you push your left leg forward with the insteps pointing forward (heels forward and elastic knees-see 'Straight Sequence'). Your opposite hand pulls your partner and lifts him as your elbow presses up under his shoulder. Keeping a strong pull, you push your bent blocking leg close alongside your partner's leg as far to the rear as possible. The knee is pointing downwards and you place only the ball of your foot down. (Take care not to let your upper body tip to one side, so that later on you are still able to put your weight on your blocking leg). You can now throw him by pushing the elbow of your opposite hand into your partner's shoulder, pulling at the same time with the other hand and finally stretching out your blocking leg.

5.3 Yellow/Orange Belt

Exercise 1
With a TAI OTOSHI, in which direction do you try to put your partner off-balance? In which direction does your pulling hand move?

_____
_____
_____
_____

Exercise 2
Which throws are illustrated in Pictures 1 and 2? What are the similarities?

_____
_____
_____
_____

Exercise 3
Your partner is standing with his right foot forward. Draw the different directions, in which you most easily throw him. Why is it easy to use these particular directions to throw?

_____
_____
_____
_____

Exercise 4
Your vocabulary exercise: What do OTOSHI, MIGI, HIDARI and KOSHI mean?

OTOSHI = _____   MIGI = _____
HIDARI = _____   KOSHI = _____

5.3 Yellow/Orange Belt

O SOTO GARI
(Major Outer Reaping)

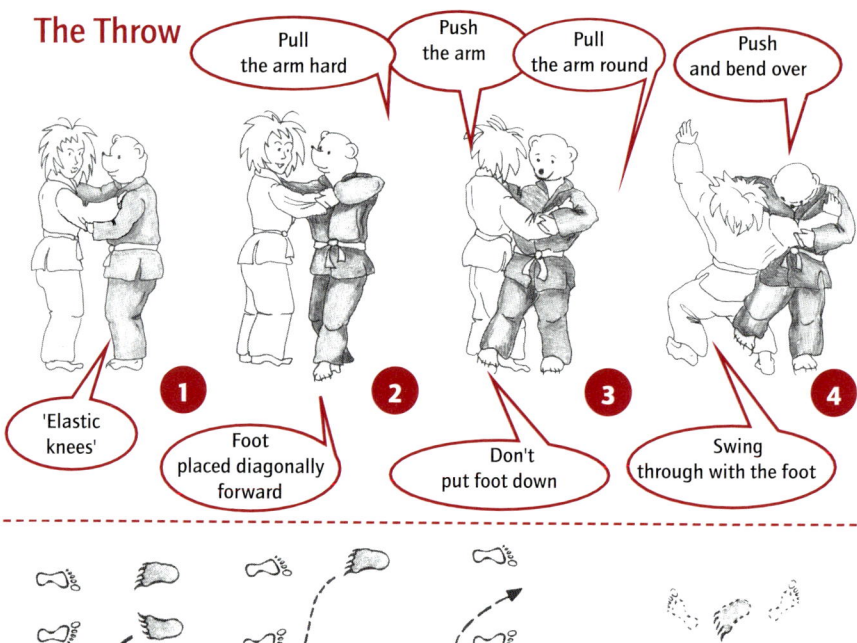

The Throw

1. Pull the arm hard — 'Elastic knees'
2. Push the arm — Foot placed diagonally forward
3. Pull the arm round — Don't put foot down
4. Push and bend over — Swing through with the foot

Sideways, sideways in you plan.
Shsst – bim – boom – bam.
On the mat down you slam.

READING NOTES:

For this throw you need to use a right-handed grip. From a sideways movement, you step diagonally forwards and pull hard on your partner. Now you pull your right foot forward and 'reap' or 'swing' – "shsst" – your partner's leg away to the rear without placing your foot down (given some practice your leg can go up so high that you end up standing on one leg balanced up). Don't forget to push and bend over your partner with your arms.

Remember:
You have already learned the O SOTO OTOSHI; in that throw you may place your blocking foot down as you reap – you don't actually reap but use the leg to cause your partner to stumble over it as you press him down with your arms.

5.3 Yellow/Orange Belt

O SOTO GARI
(Major Outer Reaping)

Exercise 1
Correctly number the sequence of foot movements for the O SOTO GARI in the four boxes below – Is the Bear UKE or TORI?

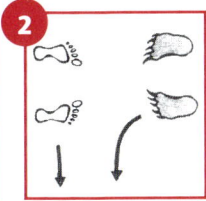

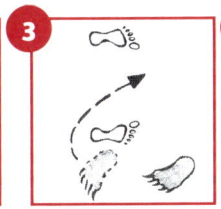

Exercise 2
Here you see parts from the drawings for the O SOTO GARI. Which drawing does each of them stem from – 1,2,3 or 4 – and what important details, that you can see in the pictures, do they remind you of? (Think of the Stardust formula...)

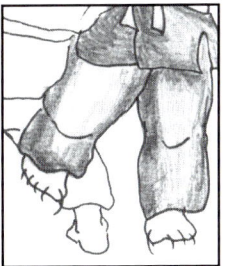

Exercise 3
Your vocabulary exercise: What do SOTO, GARI and O mean?

SOTO =
GARI =
O =

Exercise 4
What must the little Pixie watch out for when she falls down?

In what way can the little Bear make her fall more simple?

5.3 Yellow/Orange Belt

DE ASHI BARAI (Circular Motion) (Forward Foot Sweep)

The Throw

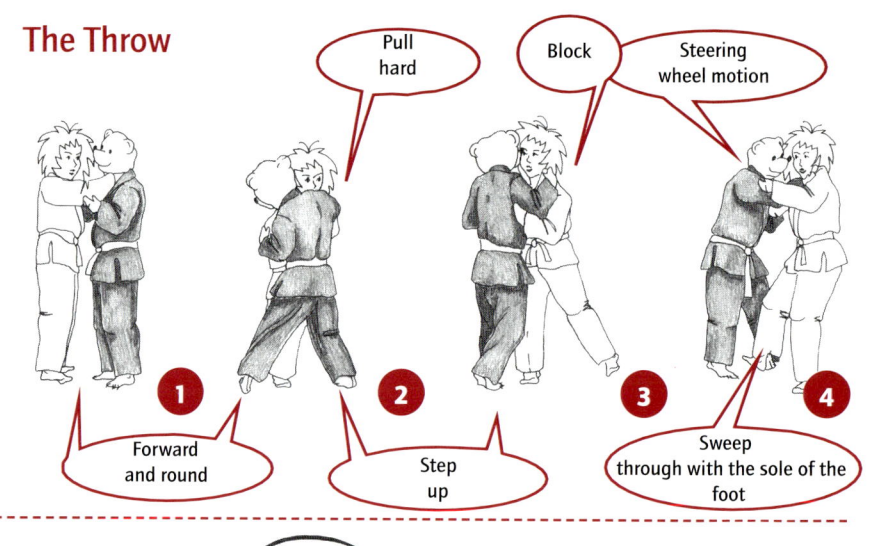

1. Forward and round
2. Pull hard / Step up
3. Block
4. Steering wheel motion / Sweep through with the sole of the foot

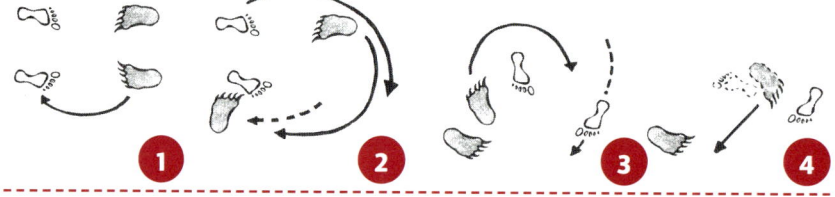

Waltz along and pull him in, with the foot around you sweep. Steer him smiling in the bin, You'll hear him surely bleat...

READING NOTES:

For this throw use a right-handed high collar grip at the back of your partner; the left hand is under his arm. Go forward with your left foot and step round (look in his ear). You place your other foot round in a semicircle behind your lead foot. At the same time you pull him in hard so that he has to take a large step in a circle. You block his circular movement with your opposite hand (steering wheel motion). As soon as your partner places his foot down and puts his weight on it, you sweep his other foot away with a long sweep of your leg (using the sole of the foot) from the rear to the front. Your arms carry on doing a steering wheel motion.

5.3 Yellow/Orange Belt

Exercise 1
Draw the correct sequence of foot movements from the circular motion for the DE ASHI BARAI (Forward Foot Sweep) in the four boxes below – also indicate which is UKE and TORI!

| 1 | 2 | 3 | 4 |

Exercise 2
Describe the role of your opposite hand in the DE ASHI BARAI. The two drawings here will help you.

Exercise 3
Which other movements can be used to employ the DE ASHI BARAI?

Exercise 4
Which other throws can be carried out from a circular motion?

Exercise 5
Your vocabulary exercise: What do ASHI, BARAI, TORI and NAGE mean?

ASHI = _____   TORI = _____
NAGE = _____   BARAI = _____

5.3 Yellow/Orange Belt
And something about competition rules...

Perhaps your feel ready enough that you would like to have a go at judging yourself in a proper competition fight with others – if only the rules weren't so confusing.

Don't worry – they aren't as bad as all that. After your weigh-in and warming up, you look for the mat area for your particular weight category and wait until your bout is called forward. Take it easy – at the right moment your trainer will turn up and will help you to get in the right place. In the meanwhile you can have a good look round.

The red square of mats is the fight area (the red mats also belong to the area) out of which you are not allowed to step. The person in the black jacket on the mats is the referee, who watches to make sure everything goes fairly. He has to make doubly sure about this because if it weren't for the competition belts, he wouldn't be able to distinguish quickly between the fighters on the mat. The first fighter called out wears the red competition belt and the second one called out the white belt.

The competition starts as the two opponents stand in front of each other, bow and then the referee says "Hajime!" Both fighters try to adopt their starting grips. If one of them manages to effect a perfect throw, so that the opponent lands on his back on the mat, the referee throws his hand up and shouts "Ippon!" (A point, victory), and then he says "Sore made" (That's all) and the fight is ended. If the throw was not quite so effective, the referee calls out "Waza-ari" (a half a point). This is also quite good, because a further "Waza-ari" added to the first equals an "Ippon", and now the referee calls out "Waza-ari awasete Ippon, sore made". This means: two half points equals one Ippon, and that means a win. Because the opponent can also do Judo – otherwise he wouldn't be standing on the mat – and he can defend himself in some way or other, not every throw comes off so well. Thus sometimes the person thrown lands on his stomach (no point), on his side ("Yuko") or on the most valued of all ("Koka").

There are also points awarded in groundwork fighting. If one fighter has managed to achieve a hold over his opponent, the referee calls out "Osae-komi" (A hold down). It now depends on how long the hold can be held. An "Ippon" is awarded for a hold down of 25 seconds. If the opponent can free himself out of the hold, the referee announces "Toketa!" (Hold down broken) – for 20-24 seconds there is after all a "Waza-ari", for 15-19 seconds a "Yuko" and for 10-14 seconds there's a "Koka". For the older age groups, arm-locks and strangleholds are allowed and can give the

5.3 Yellow/Orange Belt

fighter an early "Ippon" thus deciding the match – but for you techniques such as these are not yet allowed.

The points are shown on a scoreboard. The length of a bout can be different – for you it may be about three minutes. The clock is stopped for each break in the fight when the referee calls "Matte" (Stop, wait).

A penalty is always a bad thing – usually for the penalised person. Examples of unfair play lead to "Hansokumake" (Disqualification) – but this very rare. Small offences e.g., a fighter's inactivity are penalised by a "Shido" (a negative "Koka") or a "Chui" (a negative "Yuko"). The penalty points are transferred to the opponent as plus points. However, at your age the referee will first of all mostly give warnings and instruction because you will not be expected to know all the mistakes you make. If a bout is drawn, the referee will give the final outcome regarding who wins, and this is mainly decided by evaluating who was the most active during the fight.
 Now you have had a good look around – and your name has just been called out....

What do you do **when**:

...the referee calls out "OSAE-KOMI"?

...the referee calls out "HAJIME"?

...the referee calls out "TOKETA"?

5.4 Orange Belt

HARAI GOSHI (Hip Sweep)

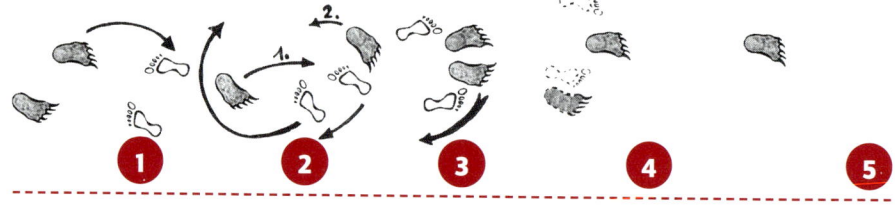

The Throw

- Lapel hand pulls round in a circle
- Grab round the hips
- Pull with the arm, look at your watch
- Turn the upper body

1. Forward and circle round
2.
3. Elsastic knees
4. Sweep with a stretched-out leg
5.

READING NOTES:

Waltz him in a circle round,
then stop him:
Sling your arm around his hip –
now sweep him high above the ground:
His stunning fall may well be steep!

Right-handed grip. With your left foot you step right forward and go round your partner. Now pull him with the lapel hand hard towards you and at the same time bring your right foot in so they come together (1) and make room for your partner to move into. You now parry his circular movement with your former lapel hand by grabbing him round the hips. Take a step back in a semicircle (look at your watch). You now start your sweeping movement towards the outside. You now throw your partner (pull and look at your watch) by bending your upper body over, turn and lift your leg up in a sweeping movement.

5.4 Orange Belt

HARAI GOSHI (Hip Sweep)

Exercise 1
Which throw is pictured here?
Describe briefly the similarity to the HARAI GOSHI.
_____
_____
_____

Exercise 2
Which throws are illustrated in Pictures 1 and 2? What are the similarities?
_____
_____
_____
_____
_____

Exercise 3
Which throws are illustrated by the Pictures 1 and 2? Describe briefly the details which are similar and then the differences?
_____
_____
_____
_____
_____

Exercise 4
Your vocabulary exercise: What do HARAI, BARAI, GOSHI and KOSHI mean?

HARAI = _____   BARAI = _____
GOSHI = _____   KOSHI = _____

5.4 Orange Belt

KO SOTO GAKE
(Minor Outer Hooking)

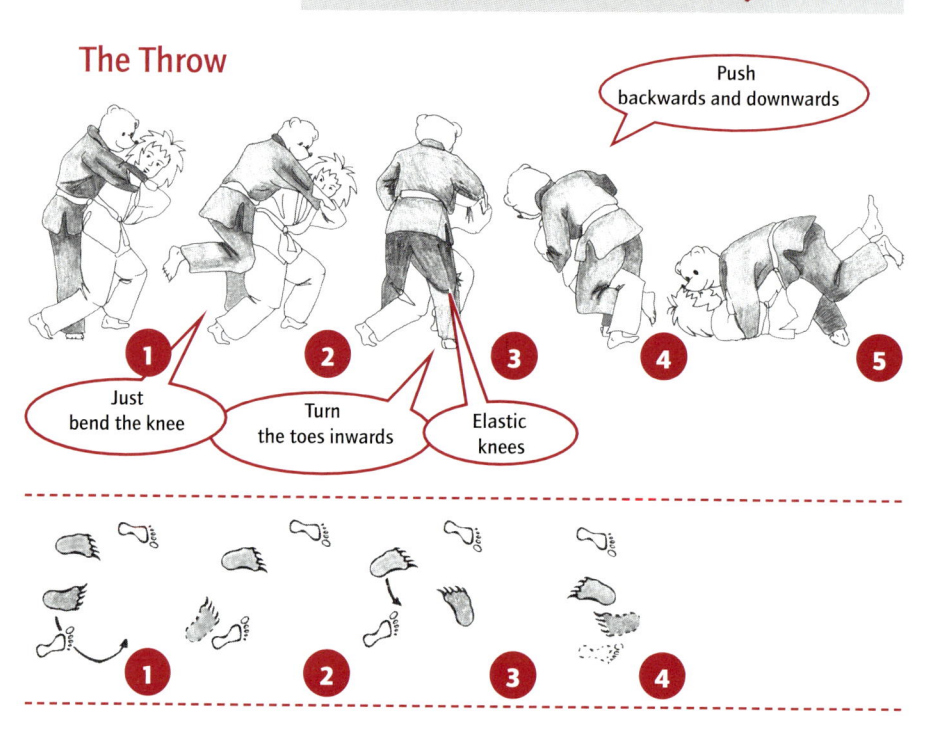

The Throw

Push backwards and downwards

1. Just bend the knee
2. Turn the toes inwards
3. Elastic knees
4.
5.

Dodge him: Swiftly bend your knee (toes inward) to your secret glee, took from outside into his leg now you can push him on his back!

READING NOTES:

Right-handed grip. When your partner just starts to turn in for a TAI OTOSHI, block the throw hard and then dodge round by climbing over his blocking leg (only bend the knee for this). The toes of the leg you climb over with turn inwards at the same time. You bend your knees (elastic knees).

For the counter throw you now push him with both arms backwards and downwards and hook, at the same time, your other leg into your partner's blocking leg. Now push energetically backwards and downwards (look towards the mat) and at the same time hook away his blocking leg with your hooked-in leg.

5.4 Orange Belt

KO SOTO GAKE
(Minor Outer Hooking)

Exercise 1
What is the difference between SOTO and UCHI? Describe briefly where you have to put your leg for the techniques which have the words SOTO or UCHI in their title?

_____
_____
_____

Exercise 2
What is the difference between KO and O? Describe briefly your leg movements for the techniques which have the words KO or O in their title?

_____
_____
_____

Exercise 3
Which throws belong to the illustrated extracts in Pictures 1 and 2? Describe briefly the details which are similar and then the differences?

_____
_____
_____
_____
_____
_____
_____

Exercise 4
Your vocabulary exercise: What do KO, O, SOTO, UCHI, GARI and GAKE mean?

O	= _____	SOTO	= _____
KO	= _____	UCHI	= _____
GARI	= _____	GAKE	= _____

5.4 Orange Belt

O UCHI BARAI
(Major Inner Sweeping)

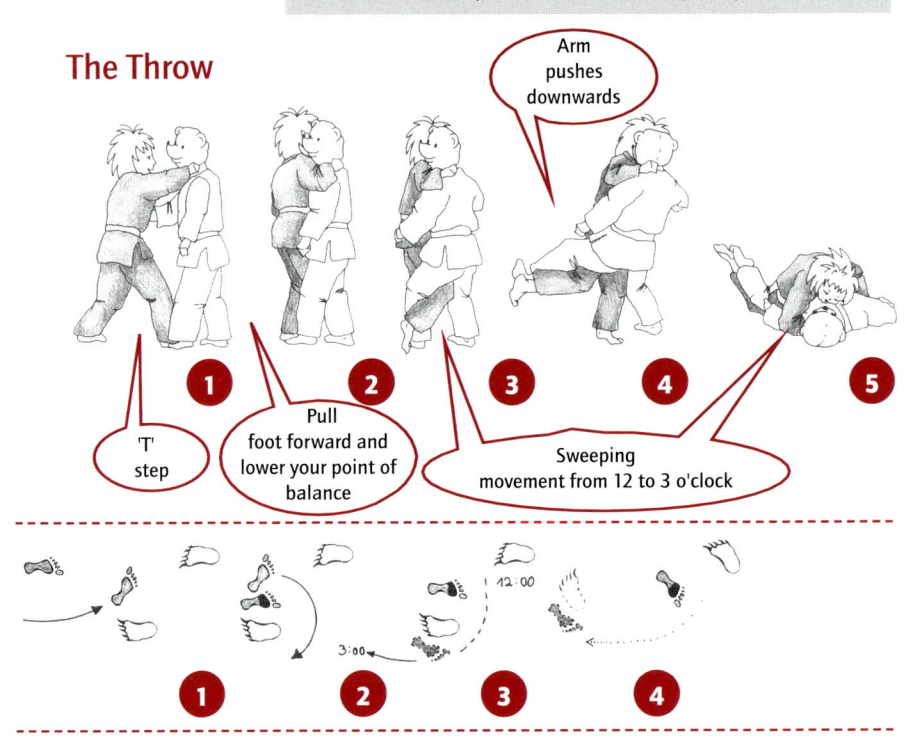

The Throw

Arm pushes downwards

1. 'T' step
2. Pull foot forward and lower your point of balance
3. Sweeping movement from 12 to 3 o'clock
4.
5.

READING NOTES:

Your partner steps right up to you, you T-step, push forward (to be true), and sweep his leg from twelve to three, backwards he goes down like a tree.

You stand with your right foot forward and take a high collar grip. Your partner takes a long step forward. You then make a 'T' step forward and pull like for the KODOKAN sequence. Step up with your left leg. Don't forget to bend your knees (elastic knees) at the same time. As both your arms push down and backwards, you sweep, from the hips, your partner's legs away in a movement from 12 to 3 o'clock. As you do this look down forward at the mat.

Tip for the advanced student:
If UKE's leg is unweighted, TORI should use a sweeping (BARAI) movement, if UKE's leg is weighted, TORI should use a reaping (GARI) movement.

5.4 Orange Belt

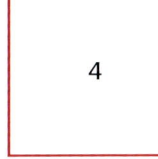

O UCHI BARAI
(Major Inner Sweeping)

Exercise 1
Cut out the pictures at the bottom of this page and stick them in the squares in the right order.

| 1 | 2 | 3 | 4 |

Cut out the pictures of the feet, shown at the bottom of this page, put them in the correct footprint sequence and stick them in the squares.

| 1 | 2 | 3 | 4 |

Exercise 2
What do you have to remember when you execute an O UCHI BARAI throw? (Remember the 'Stardust' rhyme).

_____

_____

Exercise 3
Your vocabulary exercise: What do O, KO and BARAI mean?

O = _____
KO = _____
BARAI = _____

Exercise 4
What do you do when you have carried out an O UCHI BARAI during a RANDORI ?.

○ Eat an ice-cream
○ Take a grip-hold
○ Run to Mummy
○ Stand up and try again

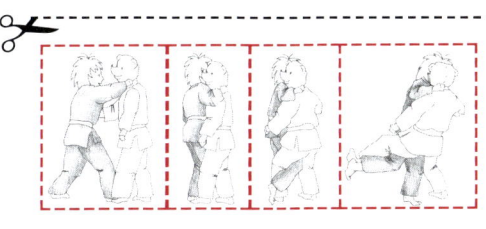

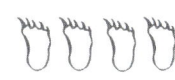

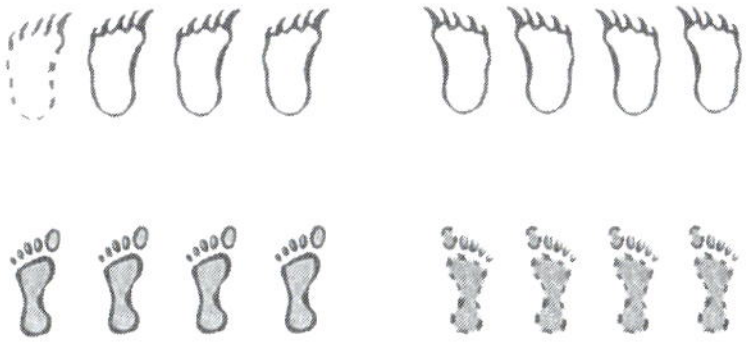

5.4 Orange Belt

KO UCHI BARAI
(Minor Inner Sweeping)

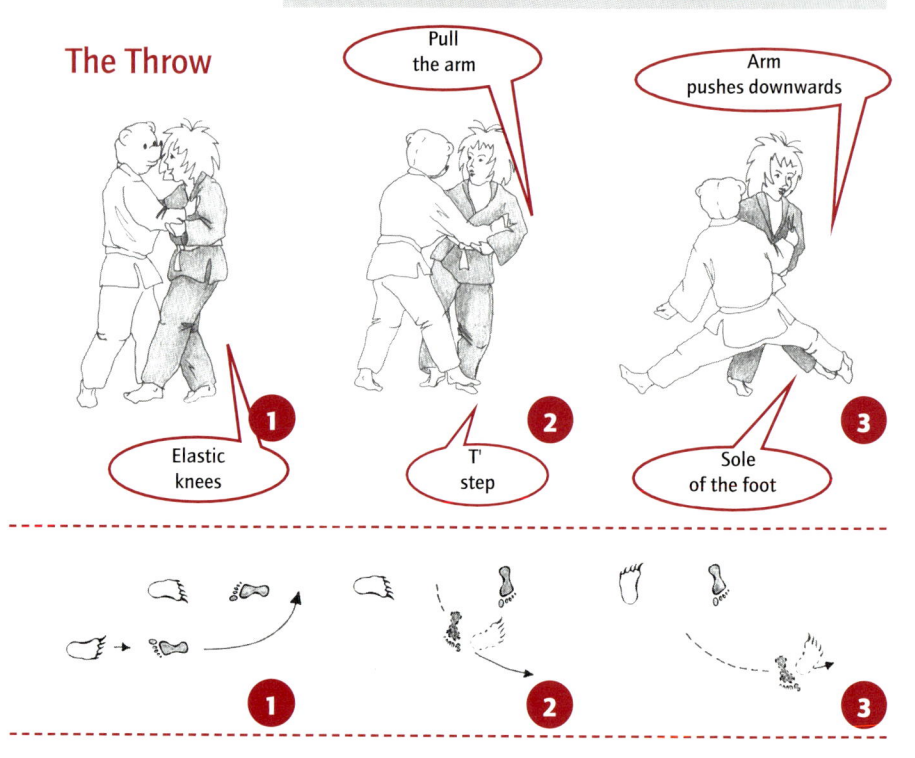

The Throw

Pull the arm

Arm pushes downwards

1 Elastic knees

2 'T' step

3 Sole of the foot

Make him take a forward step by hefty pulling on the chap, T-step and sweeping move around push him this moment on the ground.

READING NOTES:

Right-handed grip. You make your partner take a long step forward by using a hefty pull of the arm.

You use this moment to bring your foot quickly round and set it down in a 'T' step.

Just before your partner puts his foot down, you sweep his leg away with an inside movement using the sole of your foot. At the same time you push down with both of your arms.

5.4 Orange Belt

KO UCHI BARAI
(Minor Inner Sweeping)

Exercise 1
Cut out the pictures at the bottom of this page and stick them in the squares in the right order.

Throw

| 1 | 2 | 3 |

| 1 | 2 | 3 |

Feet

Exercise 2
What do you have to remember when you execute an KO UCHI BARAI throw? (Remember the 'Stardust' rhyme).

_____
_____
_____
_____

Exercise 3
Your vocabulary exercise: What do KO, UCHI and BARAI mean?

KO   = _____
UCHI = _____
BARAI = _____

5.4 Orange Belt

SASAE TSURI KOMI ASHI
(Supporting Foot Lift-Pull Throw)

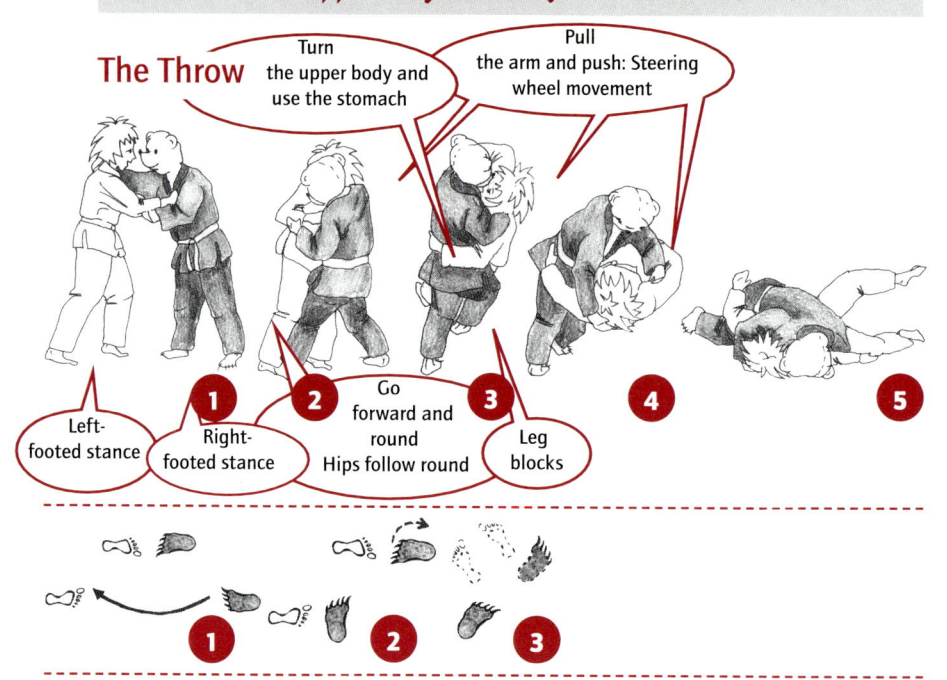

The Throw

- Turn the upper body and use the stomach
- Pull the arm and push: Steering wheel movement

1. Left-footed stance
2. Right-footed stance
3. Go forward and round — Hips follow round
4. Leg blocks
5.

With a step close in on him,
toes pointed inwards nice and trim,
Steer him round your body past,
Your blocking leg to stop him fast.

READING NOTES:

Use a right-handed high collar grip. You stand with your right foot forward. Your partner has his left foot forward and is pushing lightly. Taking a large step forward you move inside close to his rear foot with your toes pointing inwards. NB: At the same time you bend your knees (elastic knees) and move your hips in the same direction. With the hand on his collar you pull your partner towards your shoulder while at the same time your other hand pushes his elbow backwards and up (steering wheel movement). You use your stomach and upper body movement at the same time to gain more spin. Your stretched-out leg now stops your partner's leg so that he will stumble – you are still doing the steering wheel movement. You control his fall right down to the ground. Your partner must resist temptation to support his fall with his left (free) elbow.

5.4 Orange Belt
SASAE TSURI KOMI ASHI
(Supporting Foot Lift-Pull Throw)

Exercise 1
You have carried out a SASAE TSURI KOMI ASHI. Describe how you use your left and your right arm in the throw.

_____
_____
_____

Exercise 2
Out of which other movement have you already learned the SASAE TSURI KOMI ASHI? What differences occur to you (Grip, direction of the throw).

_____
_____
_____

Exercise 3
Which throws do the movements in the illustrations in pictures 1 and 2 belong to? Describe briefly the details, which are similar and then those, which are different.

_____
_____
_____
_____
_____
_____
_____

Exercise 4
Your vocabulary exercise: What do SASAE, ASHI, BARAI and SEOI mean?

SASAE = _____   BARAI = _____
ASHI = _____   SEOI = _____

5.4 Orange Belt

PRACTICE MAKES PERFECT
(or: Something about motivation ...)

"I like Judo. It's a very fair sport. Training is also a lot of fun, because we do all sorts of things like press-ups, Randori and lots besides. If you take part in a competition and lose a fight it's not bad at all. But when you win a fight, then you feel a lot of joy deep down in your heart. To take part is the most important thing."

"To take part is the most important thing." This is what one of our pupils wrote about Judo. He had taken part in a number of competitions for his age group. This says it all regarding what one can say about competitions.

Even if you don't have exactly the success you wished for in your first competition, it can't be that bad, can it? Surely it is already something to just take part? But you must not simply lose heart. At least you have gained one thing over other people: the wish and the determination to have a go sometime and take someone on. There is no such thing as "I can't do it". It's more like "I can't do that yet". So just keep on training and practising hard.

Work on those techniques that you have yet to learn new or improve, and try to get the most out of every training period. You might even, perhaps out of pure interest, be working on your sport outside the training sessions. For example you might be looking at a book to refresh your mind about techniques you've learned already. Or do you keep a sports training diary?

Sometimes it's not as simple as it sounds to get over taking it easy. Training is hard work – running makes you out of breath, gymnastic exercises cost a lot of sweat. Stretching exercises can, on the other hand, easily be faked. It's sometimes much more interesting, just when the trainer is explaining something, to chat with your neighbour and to fall into temptation to make a date to play or to swap the latest joke..... But it's just as likely that at that very moment you will have missed the most important point that would have perhaps helped you in your next Randori.

You then have to remember the correct training sequence yourself and that's a lot more difficult than when the trainer is calling out what you have to do. He can show you everything and offer helpful advice, but the degree of accuracy and intensity in the way in which you imitate and practice what you have been shown,

5.4 Orange Belt

PRACTICE MAKES PERFECT
(or: Something about motivation ...)

is up to you alone. But if you manage to overcome your own natural indolence, then you will have won the most important fight; the fight against yourself. And this will help you in many other things in later life.

Write down here those techniques, which are your favourites and what you are good at in them or what you have to still practice. Which situations do you use them in a Randori?

My favourite techniques: I can do this well: I have to improve the following:

5.5 Orange/Green Belt

KO UCHI MAKI KOMI
(Minor Inner Wrap Around Throw)

The Throw

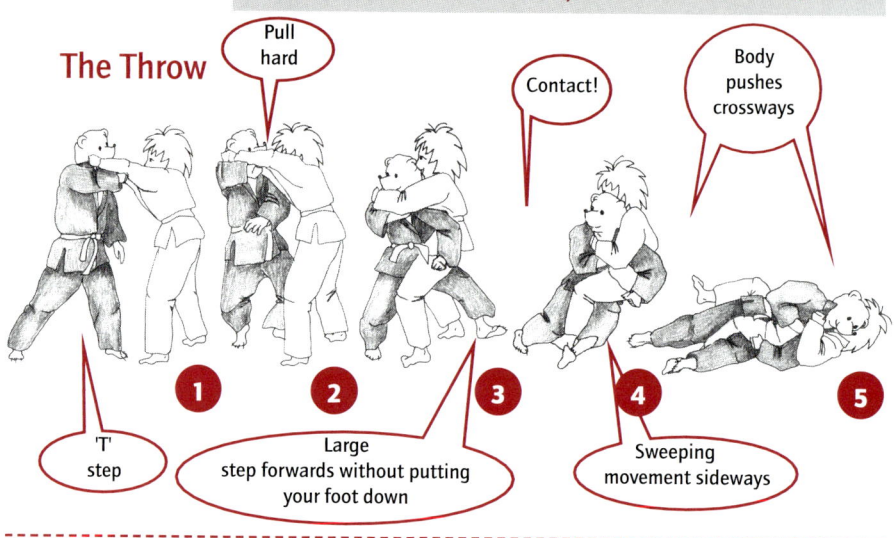

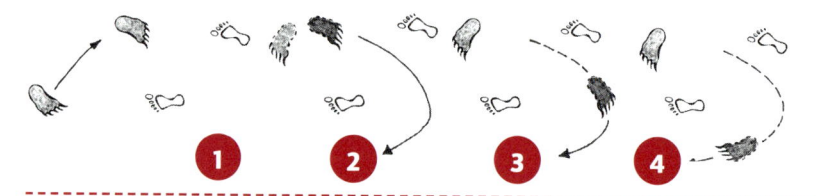

- Pull hard
- Contact!
- Body pushes crossways

1. 'T' step
2. Large step forwards without putting your foot down
3.
4. Sweeping movement sideways
5.

READING NOTES:

Use a right-handed grip. You pull your partner and place you foot down at a 'T' angle as if you were doing a SEOI NAGE (feinting). When your partner reacts to go back in order to defend against the SEOI NAGE, you pull your other foot alongside. Lay your left arm over your partner's thigh. This causes the whole of your left side of the body to come into contact with your partner. At the same time you take a large step forward without putting your foot down and now sweep his leg with a large sweeping movement sideways. Simultaneously you push your body further against your partner until he falls down backwards.

Hard you pull, 'T' step too, bring your leg round through and through. Wide step forward and swing in, sweeping his leg off as you spin. Now push him looking at the mat, you´ll land on him nice, snug and flat.

5.5 Orange/Green Belt

KO UCHI MAKI KOMI
(Minor Inner Wrap Around Throw)

Exercise 1
Briefly describe how your partner will (or will not) react when you pull him and what you then have to do. Follow the arrows.

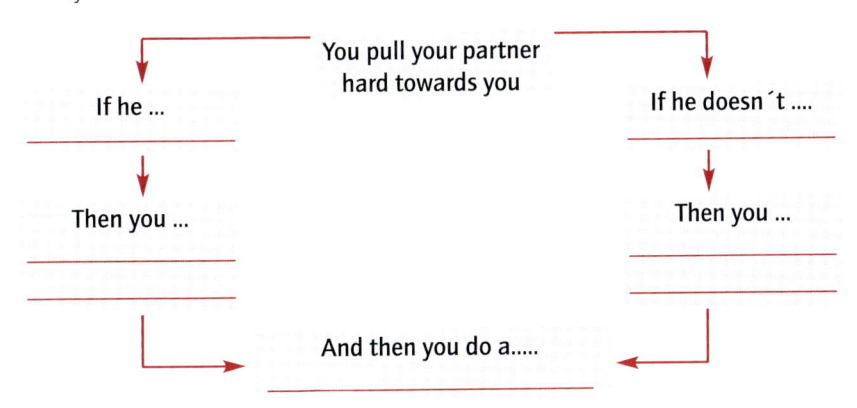

You pull your partner hard towards you

If he ...
_____

Then you ...
_____
_____

If he doesn´t ....
_____

Then you ...
_____
_____

And then you do a .....
_____

Exercise 2
Which throws do the pictures here in Figure 1 and 2 belong to? Describe the individual details, which are similar, and then the differences.

_____
_____
_____
_____
_____
_____

Exercise 3
Your vocabulary exercise: What do MAKI KOMI, SEOI, ASHI and NAGE mean?

MAKI KOMI = _____   SEOI = _____
ASHI   = _____   NAGE = _____

83

5.5 Orange/Green Belt

TOMOE NAGE (Circular Throw)

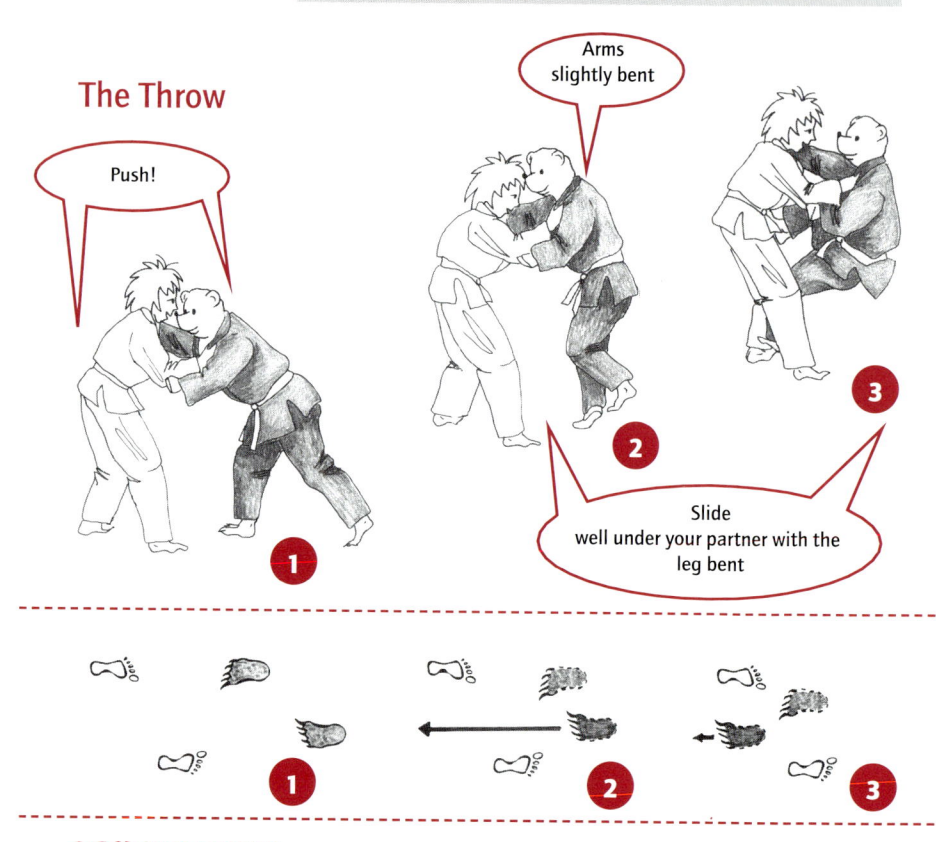

The Throw

Push!

Arms slightly bent

Slide well under your partner with the leg bent

READING NOTES:

You stand with your right foot forward and take a high collar grip. You push and when your partner reacts and pushes back (1), you pull your rear foot rapidly forward and between the legs of your partner (2,3). At the same time you place your other bent-up leg into your partner's groin (3). Your bottom slides between your partner's legs with the heel close to the leading leg (4). Make sure that you get as far under your partner's centre of balance as possible. Pull him to you hard with your arms. When your partner is above you (5), begin to stretch the leg that you have placed in his groin. Your arms control your partner as he falls (he does a big judo roll forwards). You carry out a backward roll in unison with him in order to land at your partner's side and take hold of him again (6).

5.5 Orange/Green Belt

TOMOE NAGE (Circular Throw)

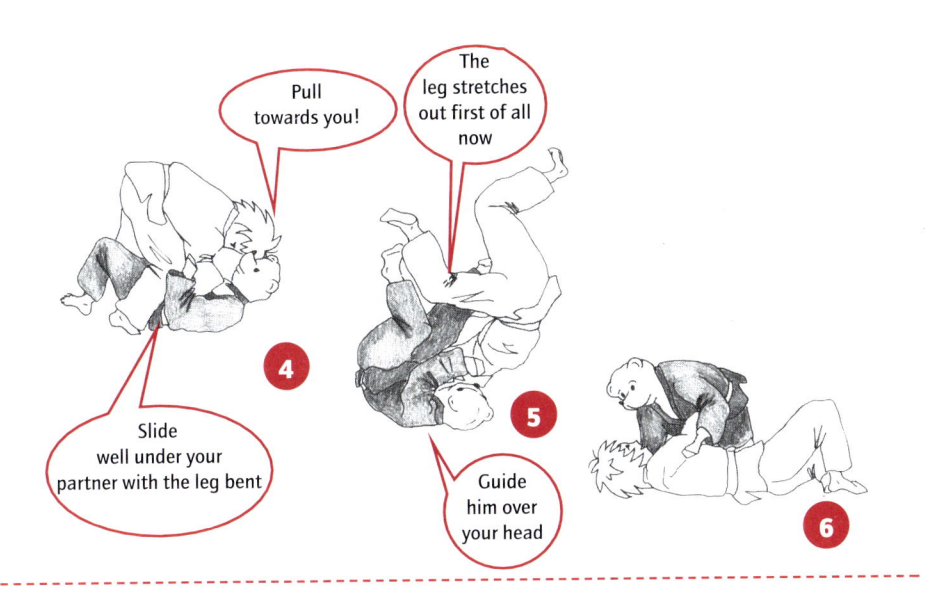

Pull towards you!

The leg stretches out first of all now

4

Slide well under your partner with the leg bent

5

Guide him over your head

6

4

You push – he pushes, and off we go;
You jump under him through and low,
leg well bent – swing bum to heel,
now leg up and push him: He will reel.
Now you roll backwards – a lovely sight –
and for a holddown grab him tight

5.5 Orange/Green Belt

TOMOE NAGE (Circular Throw)

Exercise 1
Briefly describe what work your legs are doing in the TOME NAGE. Include in particular Phases 3, 4 and 5.

Exercise 2
What role do your arms play in Phases 4 and 5 of the TOMOE NAGE?

Exercise 3
Which situations are suitable for employing the TOMOE NAGE?

Exercise 4
Your vocabulary exercise:
What do TOMOE, NAGE, KO, and SOTO mean?

TOMOE = _____
NAGE = _____
KO = _____
SOTO = _____

5.5 Orange/Green Belt

TOMOE NAGE (Circular Throw)

Exercise 5
Make yourself a TOMOE NAGE flip-book.

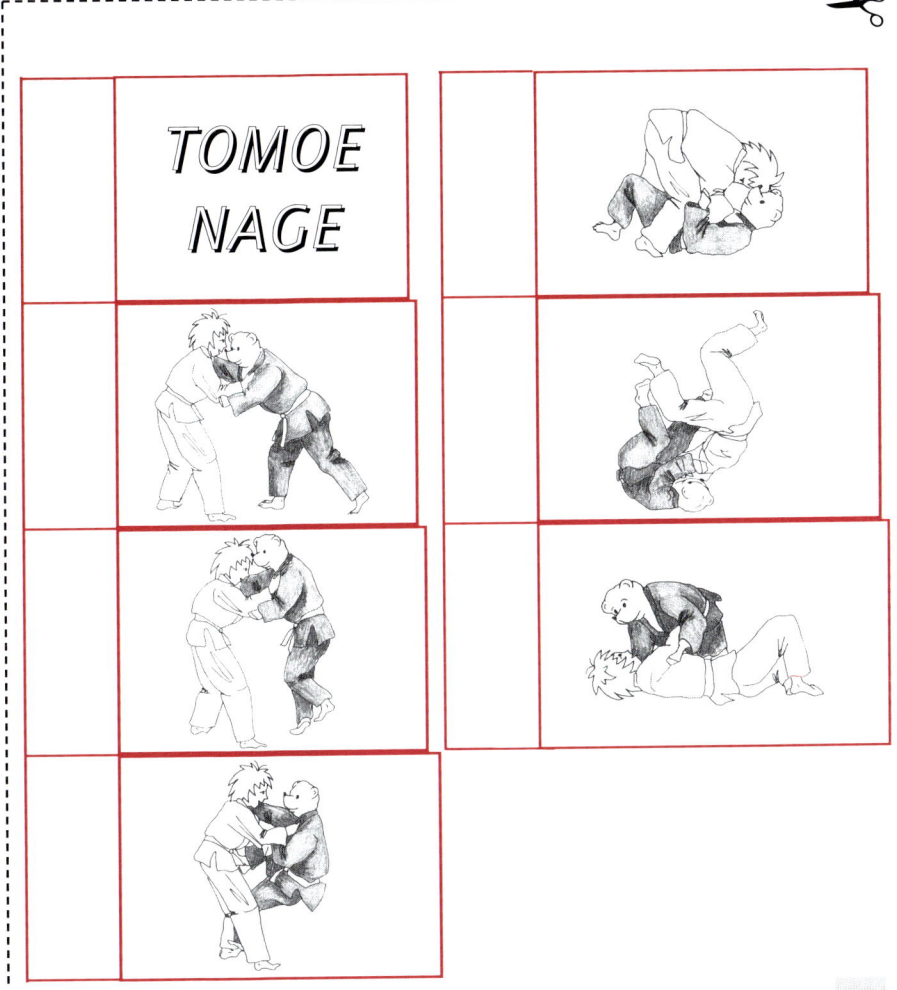

5.5 Orange/Green Belt

YOKO TOMOE NAGE
(Circular Throw to the Side)

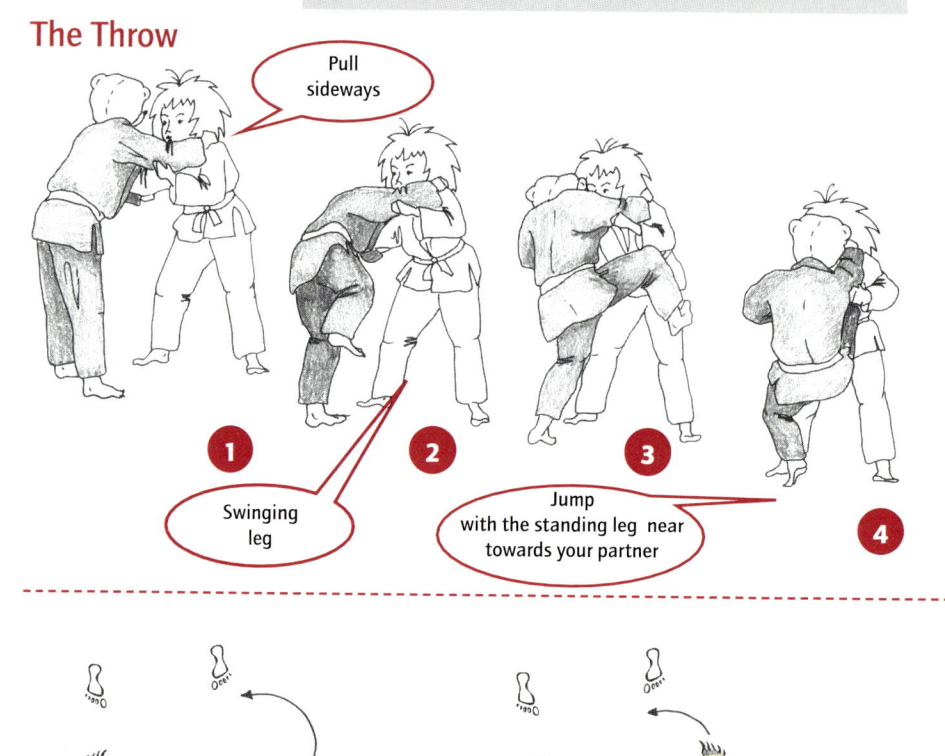

The Throw

Pull sideways

1

Swinging leg

2

Jump with the standing leg near towards your partner

3

4

READING NOTES:

You execute this throw using a right-handed grip, when your partner is standing with his right foot slightly forward. You pull by the lapels diagonally sideways until you feel him clearly resisting.

You then swing your leg from the same side in a broad circular movement, bending it up into your partner's stomach. At the same time you jump with your other leg close into your partner. You turn as you jump so that you end up lying crosswise in front of your partner. Simultaneously you push your bottom close up to your standing leg.

5.5 Orange/Green Belt

YOKO TOMOE NAGE
(Circular Throw to the Side)

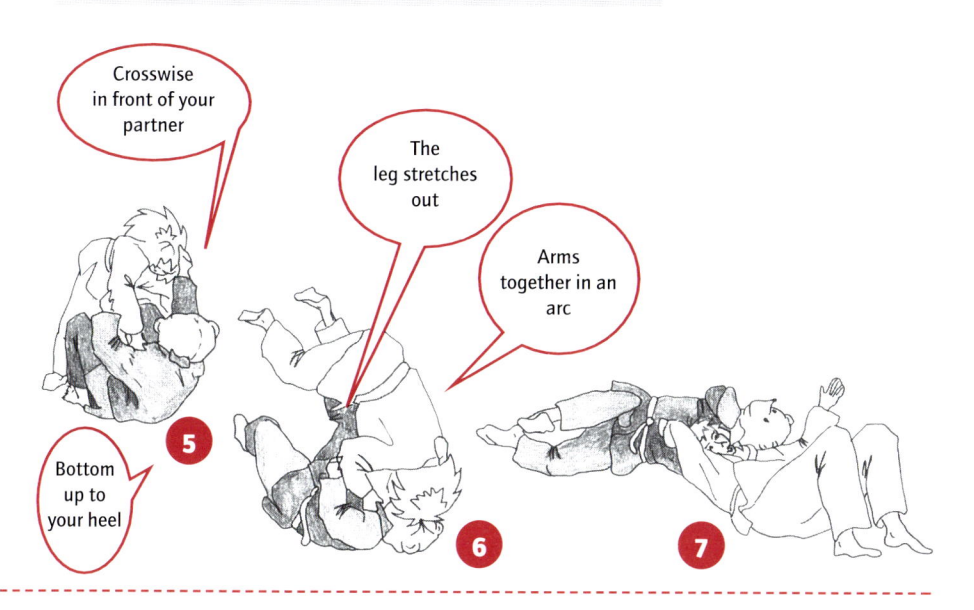

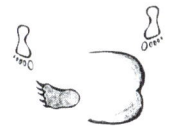

- Crosswise in front of your partner
- The leg stretches out
- Arms together in an arc
- Bottom up to your heel

As you jump forward, you pull your partner in close with your arms. You now push your partner upwards with your leg and your arms guide him in a small arc (just like in TOMOE NAGE) over your head.

You can also roll over at the same time in order to take up another grip.

Pull sidewards until he resists
as you will feel it in your fists.
With your leg now move a swing
that takes you flying like on wing
under your partner (burn to heel)
whirling him over like a wheel.

89

5.5 Orange/Green Belt

YOKO TOMOE NAGE
(Circular Throw to the Side)

Exercise 1
What does the picture on the right show and why does it differ from the YOKO TOMOE NAGE? Include in particular Phases 3, 4 and 5.

_____
_____
_____
_____

Exercise 2
Think! From which situation can you execute a YOKO TOMOE NAGE?

_____
_____

Exercise 3
Which throws allow you to prepare to be able to execute the TOMOE NAGE? i.e., which is the best situation to allow you to do it?

_____
_____

Exercise 4
You try to do a YOKO TOMOE NAGE and you get as far as lying crosswise in front of your partner, but you are not successful in throwing him over your head. What technique could you use now to follow this situation up?

_____
_____

Exercise 5
Your vocabulary exercise: What do YOKO, TACHI WAZA, NE WAZA and NAGE mean?

YOKO   = _____   TACHI WAZA = _____
NAGE   = _____   NE WAZA   = _____

5.5 Orange/Green Belt

OKURI ASHI BARAI
(Follow Foot Sweep)

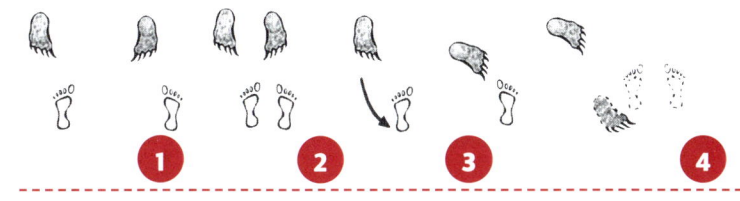

The Throw

- Arms together
- Steering wheel movement
- **1** Elastic knees
- **2**
- **3**
- **4** Leg stretched out, hips forward
- **5**

READING NOTES:

With sideways steps you move right in, elastic knees do help you spin.
Hips to the fore and sweep of the leg, twist the steering and down he's pegged

Lapel grip with left hand. You execute the throw in a sideways, lapel hand direction (1, 2). Maintain a good 'elastic knees' position. As your partner takes a step sideways, step up well into him with your toes pointing in the direction of your movement. Bring your arms together, while at the same time pulling your partner up onto the tips of his toes. Simultaneously, your other leg, stretched-out, does a sweeping movement closing your partner's legs together. The sweeping movement is complemented by the use of your hips. Your arms do a steering wheel movement as your partner is in the air.

5.5 Orange/Green Belt

OKURI ASHI BARAI
(Follow Foot Sweep)

Exercise 1
Draw the sequence of foot movements for the OKURI ASHI BARAI in the four boxes below.

| 1 | 2 | 3 | 4 |

Exercise 2
You execute an OKURI ASHI BARAI. Describe how you use your arms.

_____
_____
_____
_____

Exercise 3
Which throws are being depicted in pictures 1 and 2 opposite? Briefly describe the details, which are similar and what the differences are.

_____
_____
_____

Exercise 4
Your vocabulary exercise: What do OKURI, ASHI, HARAI and BARAI mean?

OKURI = _____   ASHI = _____
HARAI = _____   BARAI = _____

5.5 Orange/Green Belt

UCHI MATA (KOSHI)
(Inner Thigh Throw)

The Throw

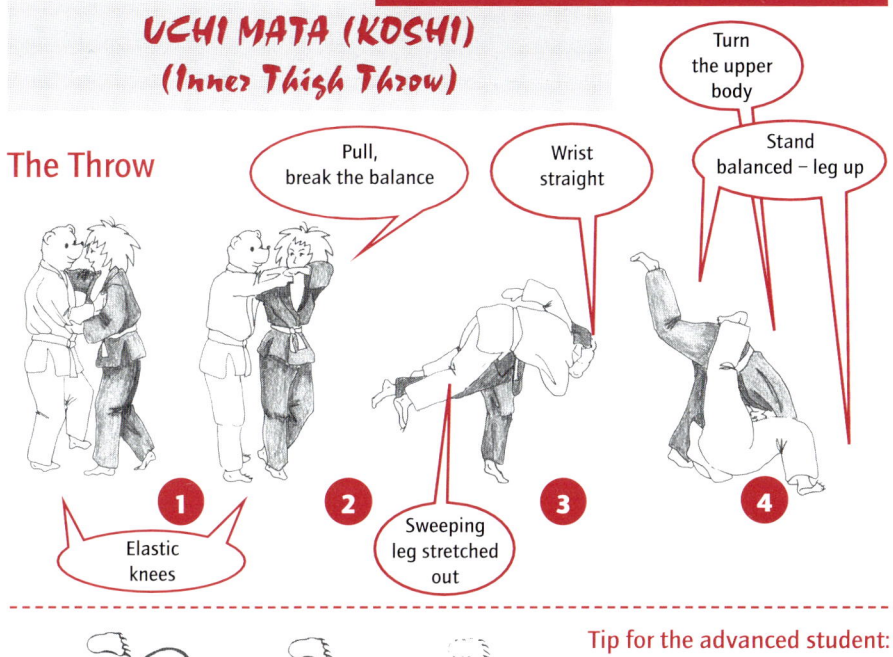

1. Pull, break the balance
2. Wrist straight
3. Turn the upper body
4. Stand balanced – leg up

- Elastic knees
- Sweeping leg stretched out

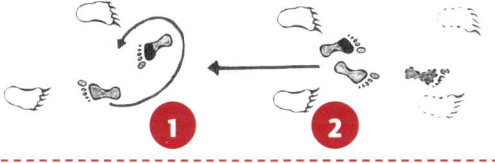

Tip for the advanced student:
Use this throw for a change out of the forward movement (KODOKAN sequence forwards)

READING NOTES:

Break his balance, then glide underneeth, (the KODOKAN sequence will guide you in this), then pull his arm like bending a bow, and swing your leg up from below, inside his legs at his inner thigh: in that way teach him now to fly!

High collar grip with the right hand. You execute the throw from a backwards direction by putting your right foot to the rear (staying on the ball of the foot) and turning it first inwards and then swing your left foot round in a half-circle. Your standing leg should be put down behind the leg you will use to sweep with later on and in a way that it touches merely with the ball of the foot. Glide down to adopt the 'elastic knees' position (KODOKAN sequence backwards). At the same time you pull your partner's arm hard (look at your watch) in order to break his balance. Your wrist – still holding your partner's collar – remains straight. Pulling hard with your arm, you bend down and sweep his inner thigh upwards with your leg stretched-out. Maintain a balanced standing position.

5.5 Orange/Green Belt

UCHI MATA (KOSHI)
(Inner Thigh Throw)

Exercise 1
What is a throwing circle?
A throwing circle is shown in the circle opposite and you can draw the throwing techniques inside it that you prefer. Imagine that UKE is standing in the upper two quarters and you are standing facing him in the two bottom quarters.

Now draw four of the techniques you most like to use. Using an arrow, indicate the direction that you will throw UKE. Label the arrow with the first letter(s) of the technique so you know which ones they are.

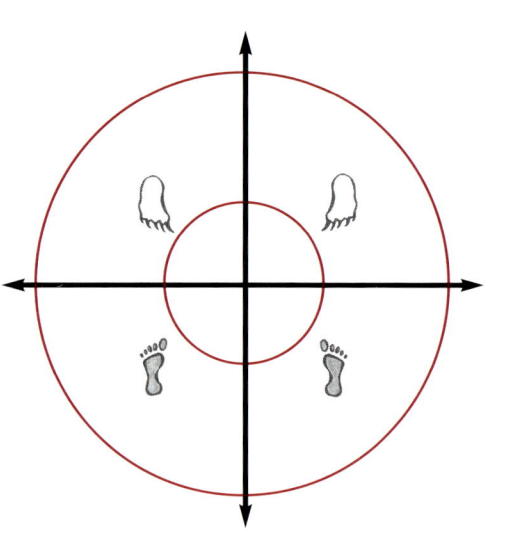

Exercise 2
Which throws are being depicted in pictures 1 and 2 opposite. Briefly describe the details, which are similar and what the differences are.

_____
_____
_____
_____
_____
_____
_____

Exercise 3
Your vocabulary exercise: What do SOTO, UCHI, MATA and ASHI mean?

SOTO = _____   MATA = _____
UCHI = _____   ASHI = _____

94

5.5 Orange/Green Belt

WHAT EVERY JUDOKA NEEDS TO KNOW

Where Judo comes from and what the word "Judo" means

In the middle-ages in Japan the **Samurai,** who were similar to our Knights, belonged to the upper social class. They had the prerogative to carry two swords and they had to follow a strict code of honour called Bushido (the way of the warrior). This social status was hereditary. However, in the course of time these 'Knights' took what they could from the ordinary people, who were not allowed to carry a weapon. Thus, the common man thought up a remedy.

One of these was found by three men in 1650, when they were told by a Chinese man **(Chen Yuanbin),** who was living in Tokyo, about a particular art where one could arrest a criminal without using a weapon. The three men – themselves "down-and-outers" i.e., out-of-work Samurai – developed from this a **system of self-defence**, which they called Jiujitsu. This word is best translated as "the gentle science" and literally it means "muscle breaking".

When Japan opened to the West (1854) the old art fell into oblivion. Everyone wanted to be modern and got themselves an expert from the West. **Dr Erwin Baelz**, a German Professor of Medicine, who was teaching at the Royal University of Tokyo, made a considerable contribution to the rise of Judo. He arranged for the old, almost forgotten art to be included as a **gymnastic exercise in the curriculum**.

Subsequently his pupil **Jigoro Kano** took up the cause and created a system (1883), which he called **Judo (the gentle way).** Contrary to the word Jitsu, which indicates a more mechanical or technical art, Judo is the term for an **ethical teaching** and imparts the sense of "the right way". Kano wished for Judo to bring out the training of the character in the human being. This was all in the way of carrying out **exercises in self-control as a gentleman, not prone to flap nor be over-reactive, who was content to follow his instructors word in a friendly manner, and who was prepared to take losing with equal calm as winning.** All a bit difficult to keep up to perhaps – don't you think?

But then, it is similarly also difficult to learn Judo. With well over a **hundred or more basic techniques (throws, lifts, grips and strangleholds), each of them having numerous variants**, there is an inexhaustible reservoir of things to be

5.5 Orange/Green Belt

taught and learn. Besides demanding physical strength, the techniques require **lithe movements at speed**, both for the surprise attack as well as reaction in defence. To be able to digest all this also demands a **mental effort. It trains the body in a form of physical intelligence.** When all is said and done, Judo is a partner sport. You can only train with a partner. Without one you will not be able to measure your own strength and skill, and you must always take care to protect him against injury.

(Printed here with kind permission of Heiner Sauer)

So – have you been paying attention?

If so, then you will surely be able to answer the following questions now:

1. What is the name of the founder of Judo?
___
___
___

2. Who were the Samurai?
___
___
___

3. List all that a Judoka has to learn...
___
___
___

5.6 Green Belt

TANI OTOSHI (Valley Drop)

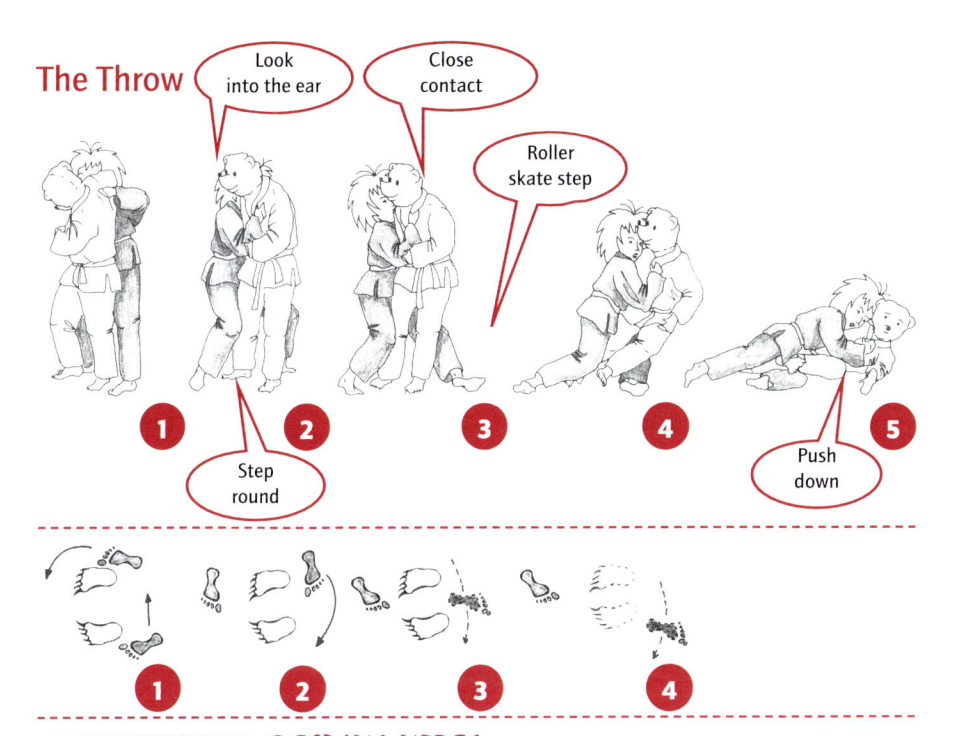

The Throw

1. (Look into the ear) (Step round)
2. Close contact
3. Roller skate step
4.
5. Push down

READING NOTES:

While your partner is trying to turn in with a hip technique, you block him (hips low and forward). Then you step round him, going deep into the knees (look into the ear). You grasp him round the hips, and with your lapel hand you push him rearwards. Your body is now in close contact with your partner's side. The leg, which is behind your partner, now glides (roller skate movement) close round your partner's leg from the rear. You now try to look over his shoulder (head on chest) and your upper body leans on your partner taking him down.

Tip for the advanced student:

This throw can be used as an attacking movement or following a feinted hip technique (front to rear).

He turns in nicely for a throw. You block him (keep your hips quite low). Now you swiftly step around, push in close contact to his side. Slip like a skater to the ground, let your leg behind him slide!

5.6 Green Belt

TANI OTOSHI (Valley Drop)

Exercise 1
Which phase of the throw is depicted in the picture? Briefly describe what you see. Why is this action important for the throw?

_____
_____
_____
_____

Exercise 2
The throw here is described as a defensive reaction to a hip throw (counter throw) How could you use it as an attacking technique?

_____
_____
_____
_____

Exercise 3
Which throws are being depicted in pictures 1 and 2 opposite. Briefly describe the details, which are similar and what the differences are.

_____
_____
_____
_____
_____

Exercise 4
Your vocabulary exercise: What do TANI, OTOSHI, MAKI KOMI and KO mean?

TANI   = _____   MAKI KOMI = _____
OTOSHI = _____   KO   = _____

5.6 Green Belt

YOKO OTOSHI (Side Drop)

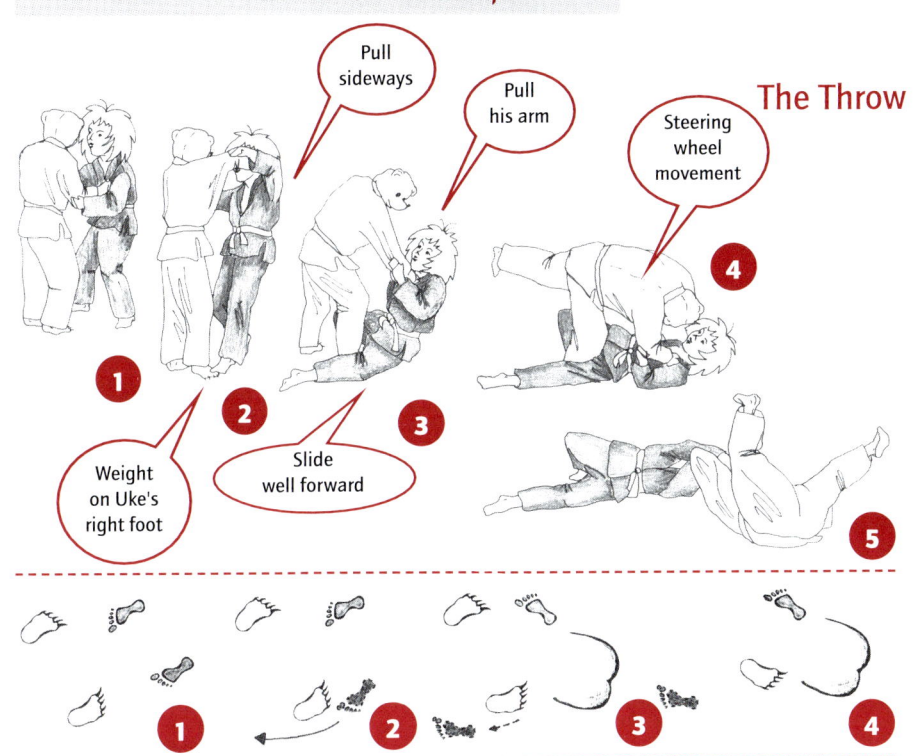

Pull sideways

Pull his arm

Steering wheel movement

The Throw

Weight on Uke's right foot

Slide well forward

Pull sideways up and swiftly dive, sliding your leg to stop his strive, now pull him down, steer him around: he will roll sideways to the ground.

READING NOTES:

Adopt a right-handed grip with feet parallel. Pulling him, you cause your partner to come forward diagonally with his right foot, thus moving the centre of his balance there. Your foot now glides forward past your partner's side, so that the inside of your upper leg blocks his forward leg. Simultaneously you pull his arm downwards. Your other hand now pushes him, so that by using a steering wheel movement, you bring him over your blocking leg. Your partner does a sideways judo roll.

Tip:
Practice the judo roll beforehand from a sideways movement.

5.6 Green Belt

YOKO OTOSHI (Side Drop)

Exercise 1
The YOKO OTOSHI belongs to your sacrifice techniques (SUTEMI WAZA). Which other sacrifice techniques have you already learned?

_____
_____
_____

Exercise 2
Try to place the sacrifice techniques that you know into the categories in the table below:

MA SUTEMI WAZA   YOKO SUTEMI WAZA
(throwing and lying down on your back)   (throwing and lying down on your side)

_____   _____
_____   _____
_____   _____

Exercise 3
In the YOKO OTOSHI, your partner falls using a sideways executed judo roll. Try to construct the YOKO OTOSHI so that it becomes a forward roll, like in the TOMOE NAGE. Tip: You can no longer lay your leg down along your partner's side, but you can... Briefly describe your throw and draw the foot movements for your throw, with your starting standing or lying position. Where is UKE standing?

Sequence of steps

_____
_____
_____

Exercise 4
Your vocabulary exercise: What do YOKO, OTOSHI, KO and O mean?

YOKO = _____   OTOSHI = _____
KO   = _____   O   = _____

5.6 Green Belt

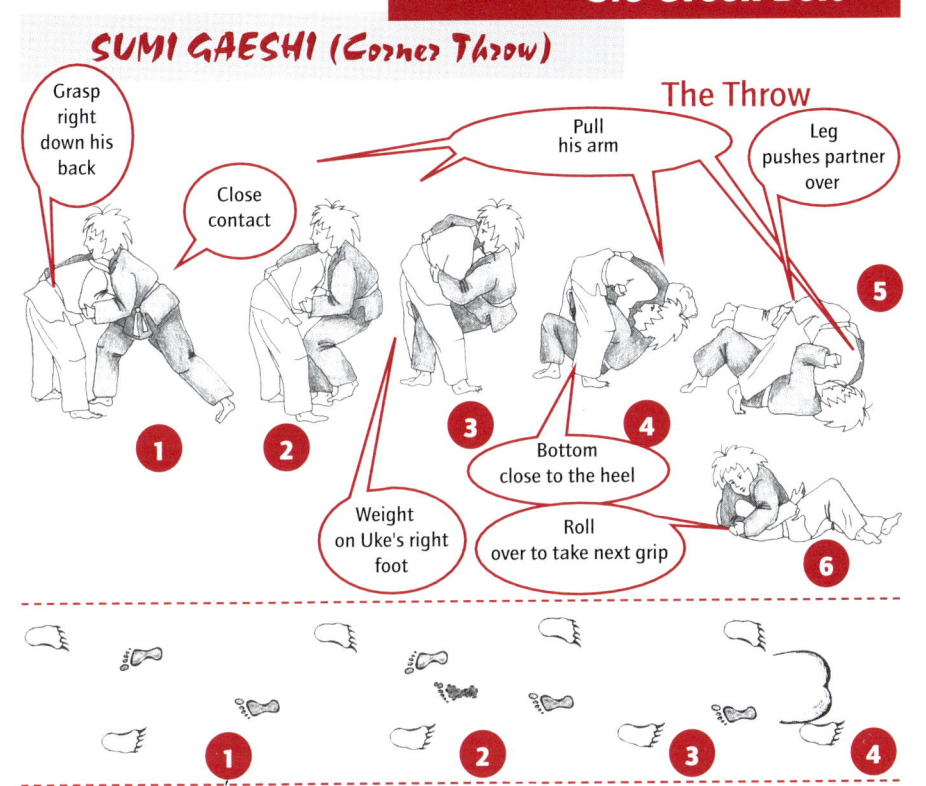

SUMI GAESHI (Corner Throw)

The Throw

1. Grasp right down his back
2. Close contact
3. Pull his arm / Weight on Uke's right foot
4. Bottom close to the heel / Roll over to take next grip
5. Leg pushes partner over
6.

READING NOTES:

Over he bends so grab him tight, snip and snap slide under him right, you pull and over your leg he goes, he's down and out as everyone knows.

Right-handed grip – your partner bends well over. With your other hand you grip past his head and well down his back as far as his belt. At the same time you take a step forward with your right foot in order to gain closer contact between your shoulder and your partner's shoulder. As you do this you pull him hard (bend your arm towards you). Continually pulling, you place your leg between your partner's legs. Using the instep of your foot you put your leading leg onto the inside of his upper leg. In this way your body swings under your partner (your bottom close up to your heel). With a further pull, your leading leg tips him in a forward movement so that you both roll over like a ball. Your partner tucks his chin well onto his chest and rolls forward so that his head is protected. You maintain your grip.

5.6 Green Belt

SUMI GAESHI (Corner Throw)

Exercise 1
Which is the best starting situation for the SUMI GAESHI?
_____
_____
_____

Exercise 2
Which throws are being depicted in pictures 1 and 2 opposite. Briefly describe the details, which are similar and what the differences are.
_____
_____
_____

Exercise 3
Besides the MA- and the YOKO SUTEMI WAZA, there are three further throwing groups: TE WAZA (hand techniques), ASHI WAZA (foot techniques) and KOSHI WAZA (hip techniques). To which group does the SUMI GAESHI belong?
_____

Exercise 4
What does the SUMI GAESHI have to do with a ball?
_____
_____
_____

Exercise 5
Your vocabulary exercise: What do the following words mean?

TE   = _____   WAZA = _____
SUTEMI = _____   SUMI = _____
ASHI   = _____   KOSHI = _____

5.6 Green Belt

HANE GOSHI (Spring Hip Throw or "Spring Waist")

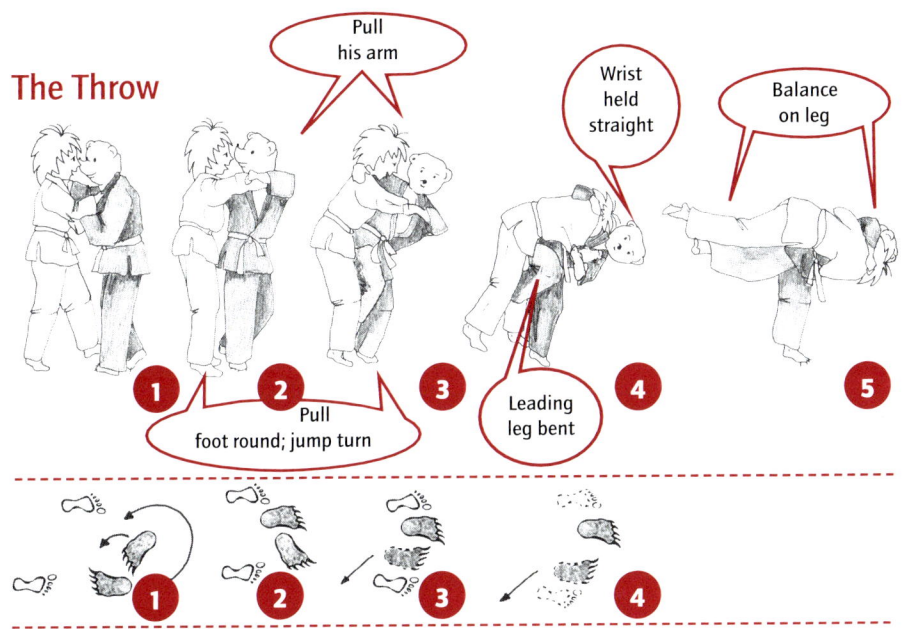

The Throw

- Pull his arm
- Wrist held straight
- Balance on leg
- Pull foot round; jump turn
- Leading leg bent

1　2　3　4　5

READING NOTES:

With a KODOKAN move get ready to start, with a jump move into him nice and smart, you pull, and your leg sweeps him away up high, like a spring you make him fly.

High collar grip with right hand. You execute the throw from a backwards direction by putting your right foot to the rear (staying on the ball of the foot), and then you swing your left foot round in a tight half-circle. Your standing leg should be put down behind the leg you will use to sweep with so that it merely touches with the ball of the foot. Glide down to adopt the 'elastic knees' position (KODOKAN sequence backwards). After a little practice, you can carry these steps out as a jump. At the same time you pull your partner's arm hard (look at your watch) in order to break his balance and to make contact with the whole of the side of your body with your partner. Your wrist – still holding your partner's collar – remains straight. Pulling hard with your arm, you bend down and sweep his inner thigh upwards with your leg bent at first and then stretched out in a spring-like movement. Maintain a balanced standing position. At the same time your upper body turns to carry out the throw.

5.6 Green Belt
HANE GOSHI (Spring Hip Throw or "Spring Waist")

Exercise 1
Which phase of the throw is depicted in the picture extract? Briefly describe the movement of the legs in the HANE GOSHI.

_____
_____
_____
_____

Exercise 2
Which throws are being depicted in pictures 1 and 2 opposite. Briefly describe the details, which are similar and what the differences are.

_____
_____
_____
_____
_____

Exercise 3
The HANE GOSHI belongs to the KOSHI WAZA (hip) techniques. Which other KOSHI WAZA have you learned up to now?

_____
_____
_____

Exercise 4
Your vocabulary exercise: What do GAKE, GARI, GOSHI and GAESHI mean?

GAKE   = _____   GARI   = _____
GOSHI = _____   GAESHI = _____

5.6 Green Belt

THE BELT HOLDS THE JACKET TOGETHER

So now you've got so far and next, you want to do your grading test for the green belt. You've got the hang of the techniques, and despite a few butterflies in the stomach, you reckon you can achieve a lot. You've worked your way up from the white belt, through white/yellow, yellow, yellow/orange and on to the orange belt, and secretly you are quite sure that shortly the blue and brown belts will follow....

But have you ever given it thought of how much your body has learned and put up with all through this time. When you began, perhaps you weren't even able to do a forward roll properly, and it was your instructor who, with a lot of encouragement, taught you to perfect this. Today you have fun doing your gymnastics and in the warm-up phase you do everything that is required, both sides of the coin so to speak – eh? You have built up strength and gradually gained the wiriness to be able to do all these exercises, and you have learned new movements and actions. At the same time your judo techniques have become gradually more perfect and today it is easy for you to do, what at the beginning was so difficult for you despite all your efforts. But you have also learned that in order to do all the exercise and learn things together, you need to have a good partner, to whom you have to have the greatest respect and demonstrate to him politeness. This begins by having your fingernails cut short and clean feet when you go on the mat, because you don't want to injure others or yourself. A clean judo suit is also not out of place – after all nobody wants to exercise with a scruffy, smelly person.... When training for the techniques, you have already learned that in working together, you have to have patience and be friends with one another. Only when you help each other and show mutual respect will you gain the most advance in your techniques. And now, of course, you have the responsibility to look after younger ones than yourself in a friendly and polite manner.

In competition, naturally, it will be different. You will soon note that your opponent, even showing all respect for your lovely new belt, will make special efforts to throw you – particularly if he is not so far advanced as you – as you will note from the colour of his belt. Also younger fighters can perhaps achieve more than you imagine, so don't underestimate anyone. Don't rely simply on the colour of your belt: the important thing is what is inside the jacket and not what holds it together!!

Test your knowledge:
Listed here are throwing terms, which have got all mixed up. Can you sort them out? (Tip: cross out the words that have already been used! You must end up with eight throws.) KO SOTO ASHI – SASAE SEOI GAESHI - SUMI GARI – TAI – UCHI BARAI – O UCHI NAGE – TSURI KOMI OTOSHI – GOSHI MATA – O IPPON

5.7 Blue Belt

ASHI UCHI MATA
(Inner Thigh Leg Throw)

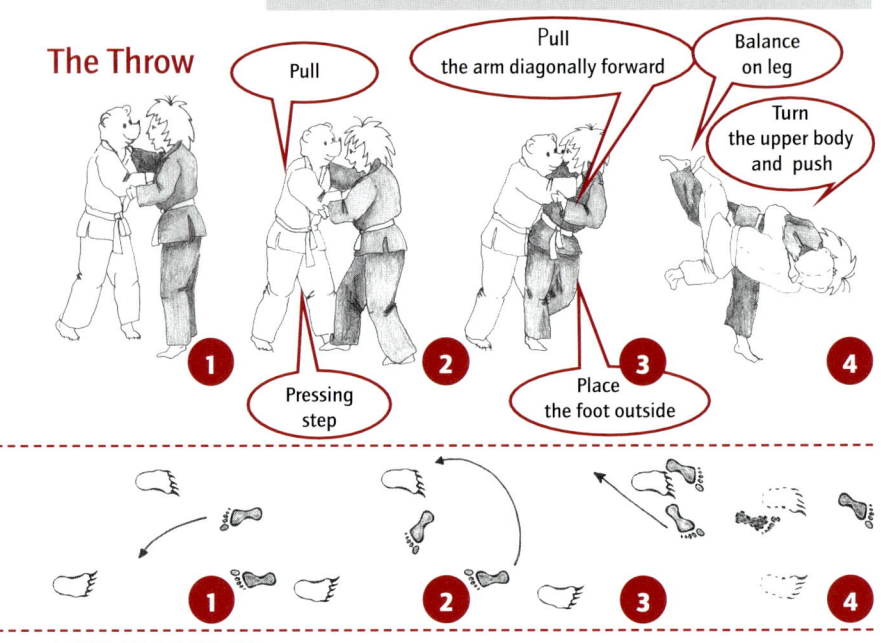

The Throw

- Pull
- Pull the arm diagonally forward
- Balance on leg
- Turn the upper body and push

1. Pressing step
2.
3. Place the foot outside
4.

READING NOTES:

You execute this throw using a high collar grip with the right hand. Your partner moves his left foot forward. You place your right leg in a pressing position forwards, right next to your partner's forward leg. At the same time you pull hard. Simultaneously your other leg swings round and is placed down next to the outside of your partner's forward leg. Using a continuous pull of the arm diagonally and forwards, you sweep the leg up, that is between your partner's, until you are balancing on your standing leg. Unlike the KOSHI UCHI MATA, your partner's left leg is swept up from the inside of his *upper* leg. Your other hand supports your pull by pressing on your partner as he goes in an arc.

Don't forget the turning movement of the upper body in order to tip your partner over. He will slip over and down like on a greasy pole.

Tip for the advanced:
If your partner doesn't go down at the first attempt, hop as you stand in the balanced position while at the same time pulling him harder and pushing him tighter (continuous attack in the KEN-KEN UCHI MATA).

> Pull, step out and sweep his thigh, thus send him flying to the sky.

106

5.7 Blue Belt

ASHI UCHI MATA
(Inner Thigh Leg Throw)

Exercise 1
Make a comparison between the ASHI UCHI MATA and the KOSHI UCHI MATA:
Which picture illustrates which throw?
Which leg is being swept away?
How is the balancing leg being placed?

_____
_____
_____

Exercise 2
You start an ASHI UCHI MATA, but you are not successful in throwing your partner. Which technique do you use to carry on with this throw?

_____
_____
_____
_____

Exercise 3
What are the possible situations to be able to start an ASHI UCHI MATA?
Which preparatory movement is best used to execute the throw (forwards, backwards, circular)? What preparatory techniques exist?

_____
_____
_____
_____

Exercise 4
Your vocabulary exercise: What do ASHI, UCHI, SOTO and SASAE mean?

ASHI = _____   UCHI = _____
SOTO = _____   SASAE = _____

5.7 Blue Belt

The Throw

O UCHI GARI (With Leg Grip)
(Major Inner Reaping)

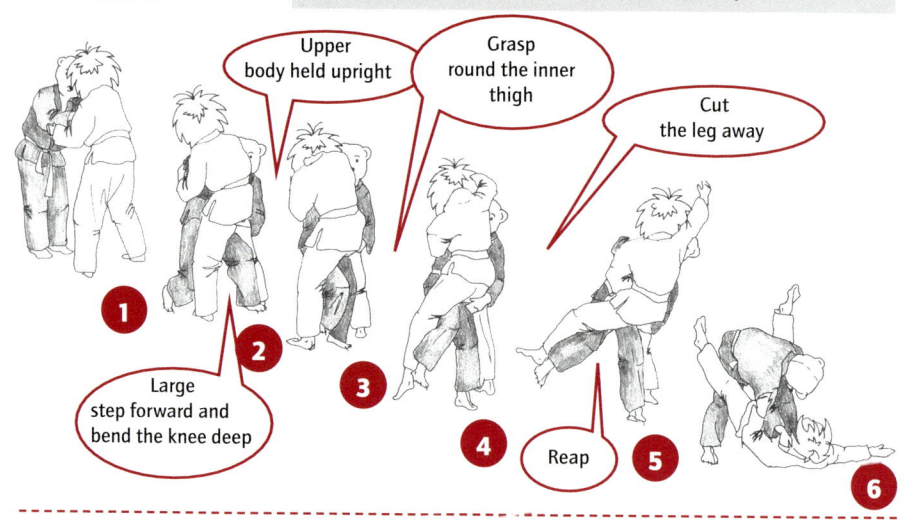

Upper body held upright

Grasp round the inner thigh

Cut the leg away

Large step forward and bend the knee deep

Reap

Step well through his legs, pull his leg back good and hard, reap round and down you peg, you've beat him – take the card.

READING NOTES:

Starting situation: A right hand grip and feet apart parallel. Using a large step forward, you duck under your partner's lapel hand and step between his legs. At the same time you bend your knees deep down and your upper body remains upright so that you achieve maximum contact with your partner.

Your left hand grasps your partner's leg from the outside and pulls his standing leg forward with force. During this you follow up with an O UCHI GARI using your other leg.
At the same time you push your partner backwards with your other hand.

5.7 Blue Belt

O UCHI GARI (With Leg Grip)
(Major Inner Reaping)

Exercise 1
Which phase of the throw is illustrated in the picture? Describe what you can see.

_____
_____
_____

Exercise 2
You want to execute an O UCHI GARI by grasping the leg. Your partner, however, leans hard forward so that you cannot throw him backwards. Which throwing options are open to you?

_____
_____
_____
_____

Exercise 3
Which throws are being depicted in pictures 1 and 2 opposite. Briefly describe the details, which are similar and what the differences are.

_____
_____
_____
_____

Exercise 4
Your vocabulary exercise: What do BARAI, GAESHI, ASHI and GARI mean?

BARAI   = _____   ASHI   = _____
GAESHI = _____   GARI   = _____

5.7 Blue Belt

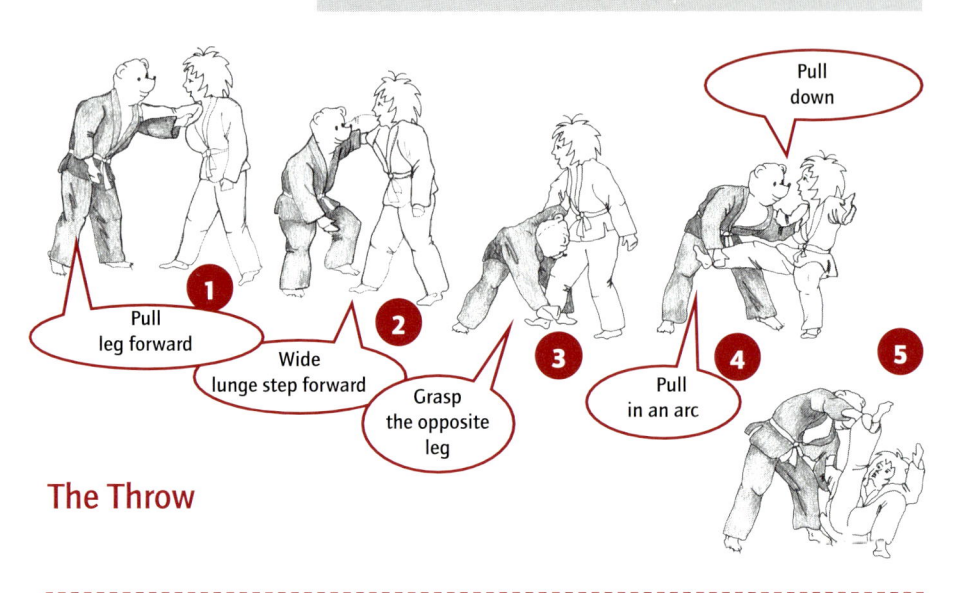

KATA ASHI DORI
(Leg Grip)

1. Pull leg forward
2. Wide lunge step forward
3. Grasp the opposite leg
4. Pull in an arc
5. Pull down

The Throw

Take a forward step, his ankle grab, and pivot him down by "pulling his leg"!

READING NOTES:

You adopt a left-footed stance and your partner a right-footed one. You are holding him on the one side by the right lapel and pull him. Pull your right foot forward and take a wide lunge step with your left leg.

At the same time you grasp your partner's opposite forward leg at the ankle and pull it in an arc.
Continue pulling in an arc and your opposite hand pulls your partner down onto the mat.

5.7 Blue Belt

KATA ASHI DORI
(Leg Grip)

Exercise 1
Describe the job your arm does in the KATA ASHI DORI!

_____
_____
_____
_____
_____

Exercise 2
You adopt a left-footed stance and your partner a right-footed one. You are holding him on the one side by the right lapel. Which options are open to you in this starting position?

_____
_____
_____
_____
_____

Exercise 3
Which throws are being depicted in pictures 1 and 2 opposite. Briefly describe the details, which are similar and what the differences are.

_____
_____
_____

Exercise 4
Your vocabulary exercise: What do UKEMI, WAZA, UCHI KOMI and OSAE KOMI mean?

UKEMI   = _____   UCHI KOMI= _____
WAZA   = _____   OSAE KOMI= _____

5.7 Blue Belt

KUCHIKI TAOSHI
(Dead Tree Fall)

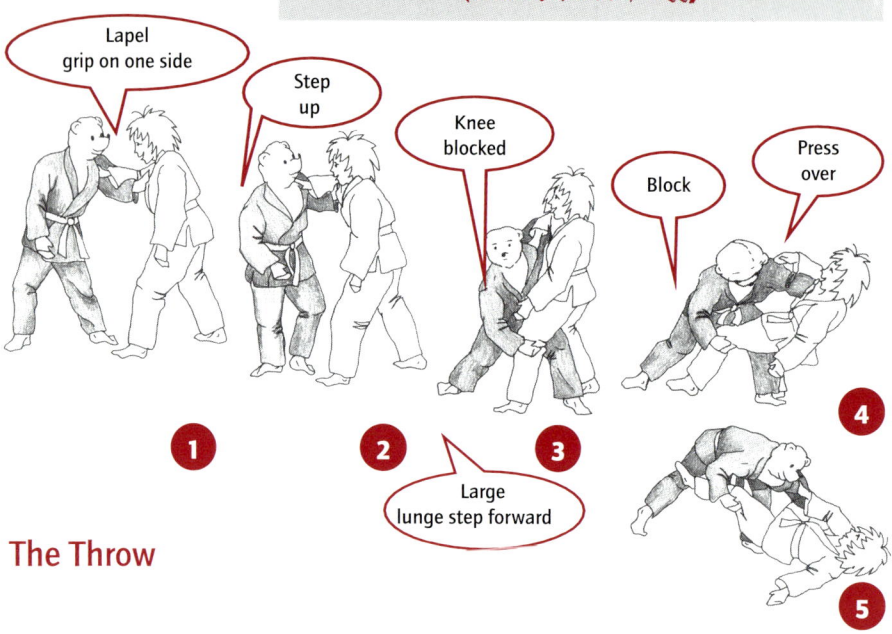

- Lapel grip on one side
- Step up
- Knee blocked
- Block
- Press over
- Large lunge step forward

1 **2** **3** **4** **5**

The Throw

1 **2** **3**

READING NOTES:

Move swiftly closer to the chap, by ringing forward in one step. Now push him back and block his knee: he´ll rumble over like a tree!

You are standing with the left foot forward as well as your partner and you have adopted a one-sided lapel grip.
You pull your partner and at the same time bring your right leg forward. Your partner reacts by going back and you use this movement to take a large lunge step forward (go deep down in your knees) between his legs. At the same time you block his knee with your free hand (grasp in the hollow at the back of his knee) and press him with force over and backwards using your lapel hand.

5.7 Blue Belt

KUCHIKI TAOSHI
(Dead Tree Fall)

Exercise 1
Why is the detail in the illustration important for the throw? Which phase of the throw is illustrated in the picture? Where does this throw get its unusual name?

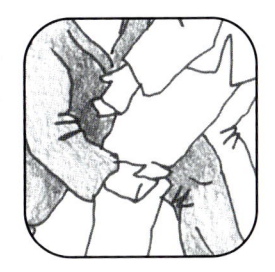

_____
_____
_____

Exercise 2
Make a comparison between the KUKICHI TAOSHI and the KATA ASHI DORI: Which picture shows which throw? Briefly describe the details, which are similar and what the differences are in the two throws.

_____
_____
_____
_____
_____
_____

Exercise 3
You have learned the KUKICHI TAOSHI. Think how a combination of the throw with the KO UCHI GARI done as a KO UCHI TAOSHI would work out. (Tip: As a comparison (see picture) remember that, just earlier, you learned about the combination of the KATA ASHI DORI with an O UCHI GARI.

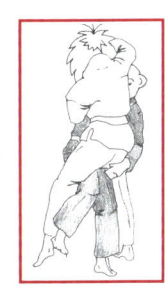

_____
_____

Exercise 4
Your vocabulary exercise: What do the following words mean?

KUCHIKI = _____   DORI = _____
TAOSHI = _____   ASHI = _____

113

5.7 Blue Belt

USHIRO GOSHI (Back Hip Throw)

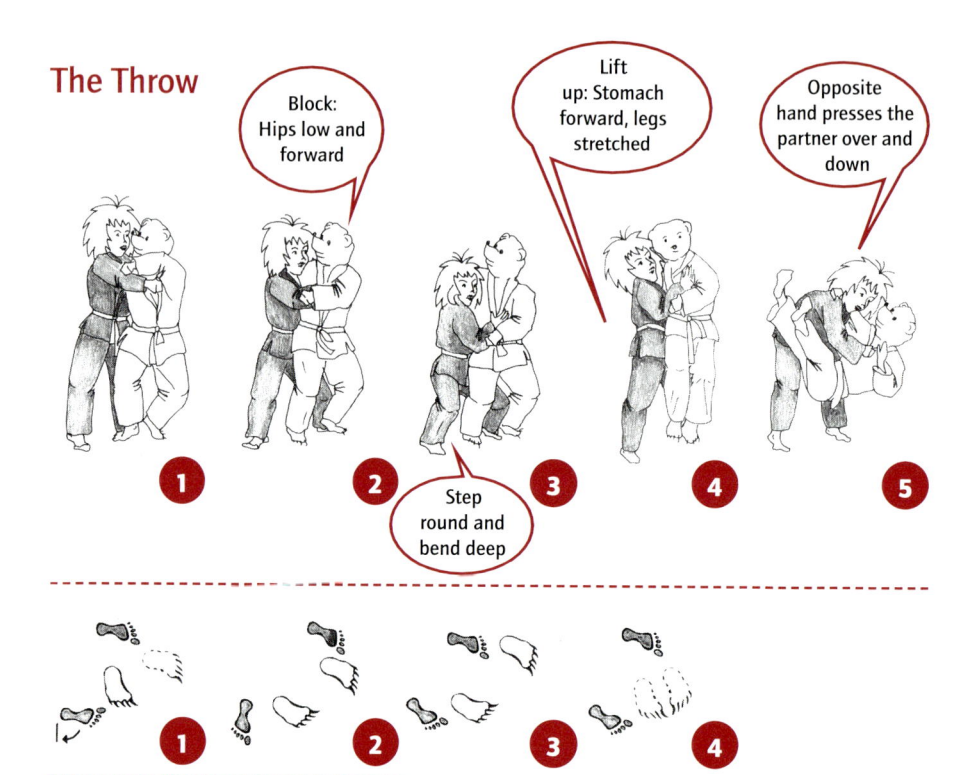

The Throw

Block: Hips low and forward

Lift up: Stomach forward, legs stretched

Opposite hand presses the partner over and down

1 2 3 4 5

Step round and bend deep

READING NOTES:

He pivots in, you block him out, hips low and forward standing stout. Now step around and lift him high, using your stomach, hips and thigh!

Adopt a right-handed grip. Your partner has pivoted in to start a hip throw. You block this by dropping down in your knees and pushing your left hip against your partner's backside. You grasp round behind your partner's hips. You step round him with your right leg. Bend down in the knees so that you get well below your partner's centre of balance.

By stretching your legs and pushing forward with your stomach, you lift your partner and press him over and down with your lapel hand so that he lands on his back in front of you. You can also take a step backwards with your left foot as you throw so that he has room, in which to fall down.

5.7 Blue Belt

USHIRO GOSHI (Back Hip Throw)

Exercise 1
Against which throws can you use this throw as a counter-attack?

_____
_____
_____
_____
_____

Exercise 2
Describe the blocking action. What are the individual details that are necessary for a successful blocking action?

_____
_____
_____
_____
_____

Exercise 3
Describe the movements that are necessary to lead up to the lifting phase. What details must be particularly noted to be successful when lifting.

_____
_____
_____
_____

Exercise 4
Your vocabulary exercise: What do USHIRO, GOSHI, KOSHI and O mean?

USHIRO = _____   O   = _____
KOSHI = _____   GOSHI = _____

5.7 Blue Belt

UTSURI GOSHI (Hip Shift)

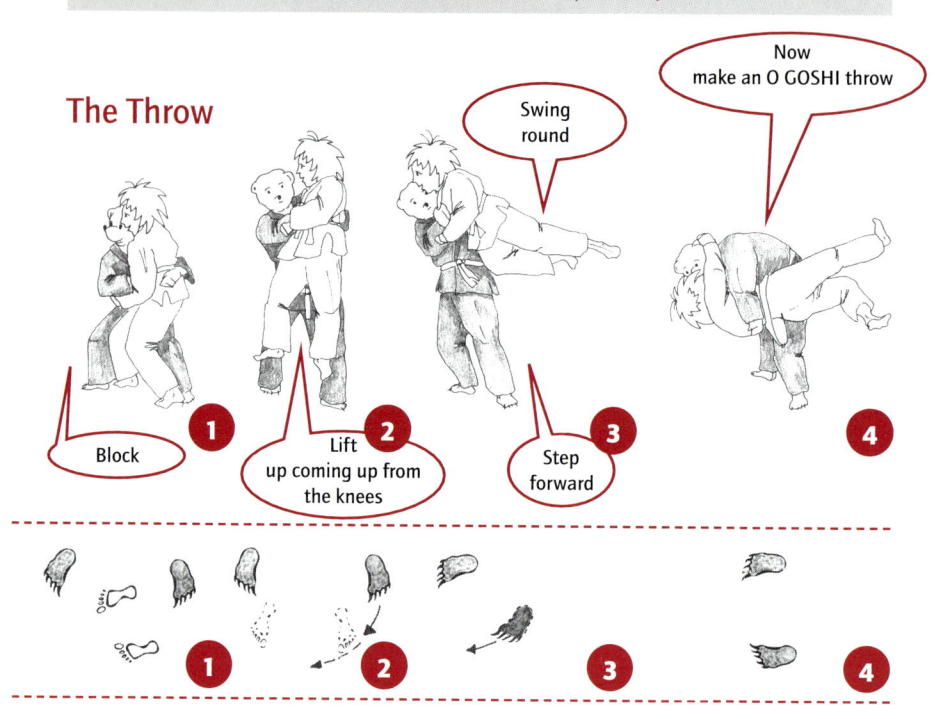

The Throw

- Swing round
- Now make an O GOSHI throw
- 1: Block
- 2: Lift up coming up from the knees
- 3: Step forward
- 4:

READING NOTES:

He starts to make a nice hip throw. So block him so he can't you know. Stomach out! You lift him right up in the air, and swing him round your hips with flair. Then take a step forward and over you lay. With a turn of your body he's on the mat to stay.

Your partner pivots in to do a hip technique. You step round him and glide down into a position below your partner's centre of balance with your knees deeply bent. You stop his throw attempts with your hips (blocking). At the same time you grasp round his hips with your left hand and your other one held against his stomach. When doing this you pull him into you. Starting down in your knees (hips forward) you lift him up and, with a steering wheel movement of your arms, you swing his legs upwards and backwards. Bring your left hip side forward and take a step forward just as you do in the O GOSHI. Now throw him by turning your upper body and bending over – and don't forget to pull with your arm.

5.7 Blue Belt
UTSURI GOSHI (Hip Shift)

Exercise 1
Which phase of the throw is illustrated in the picture?
Describe briefly what you can see.

_____
_____
_____
_____

Exercise 2
You execute a UTSURI GOSHI throw. Describe how you use your hips when blocking, lifting and throwing.

_____
_____
_____
_____
_____
_____

Exercise 3
Which throws are being depicted in pictures 1 and 2 opposite. Briefly describe the details, which are similar and what the differences are.

_____
_____
_____
_____

Exercise 4
Your vocabulary exercise: What do UTSURI, TSURI, GOSHI and O mean?

UTSURI = _____   TSURI = _____
GOSHI = _____   O   = _____

5.7 Blue Belt

TE GURUMA (Hand Wheel)

The Throw

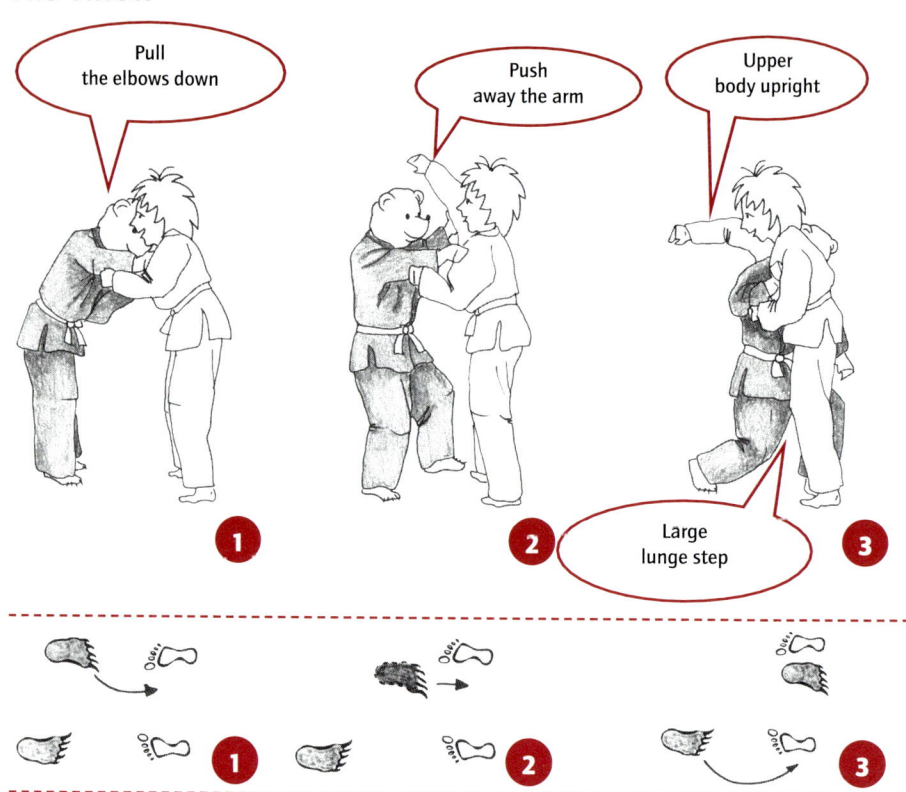

- Pull the elbows down
- Push away the arm
- Upper body upright
- Large lunge step

1 **2** **3**

READING NOTES:

Starting situation: A right hand grip and feet apart parallel. Your partner has adopted a right-handed collar grip. You pull his elbows down sharply. As he reacts with an upwards movement, push his arm up and away. You duck under his arm with your head and your arm. At the same time, your leg, on the same side, takes a large lunge step forward between your partner's legs. Watch out – Keep your back straight! Now you grasp your partner's thigh round from the outside – your neck maintains contact with his shoulder. Rising up from your legs, you lift him up by bringing your rear leg forward and pushing your stomach forwards. Your arms make a steering wheel movement in order to tip him onto his back.

5.7 Blue Belt

TE GURUMA (Hand Wheel)

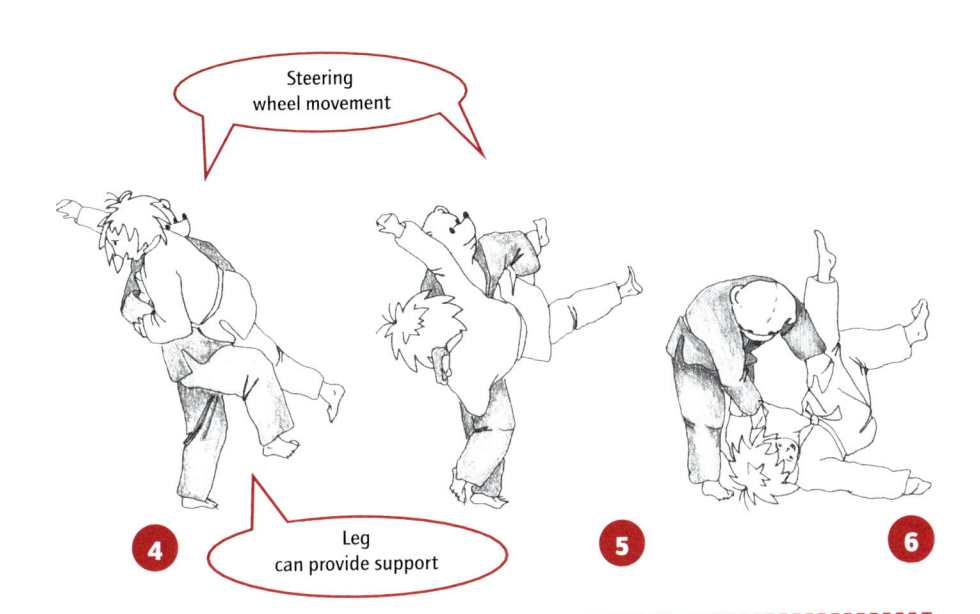

Steering wheel movement

Leg can provide support

4 **5** **6**

4

Tip for the Advanced:
Try to use your leg, as you pull forward from the rear, to support the steering wheel movement that you do with your arms (in order to sweep his legs away). In this way you will drop your partner down on to the mat.

You pull his elbow, he reacts,
now push his arm up – create some facts!
Duck underneath with head and arm,
a lunge step forward does no harm.
Then lift him up, turn him around
and send him spinning to the ground.

119

5.7 Blue Belt

TE GURUMA
(Hand Wheel)

Exercise 1
Compare picture 1 and 2: Which throw is illustrated in each picture? Describe the similarities and differences.

_____
_____
_____
_____

Exercise 2
How do you prepare for a TE GURUMA? Look at the picture on the right.

_____
_____
_____
_____

Exercise 3
Which parts of the body do the most work when lifting in the TE GURUMA throw?

_____
_____
_____
_____
_____

Exercise 4
Your vocabulary exercise: What do TE, HARA, GURUMA and OTOSHI mean?

TE   = _____   HARA   = _____
GURUMA = _____   OTOSHI = _____

120

5.7 Blue Belt

TE GURUMA (As a counter) (Hand Wheel)

The Throw

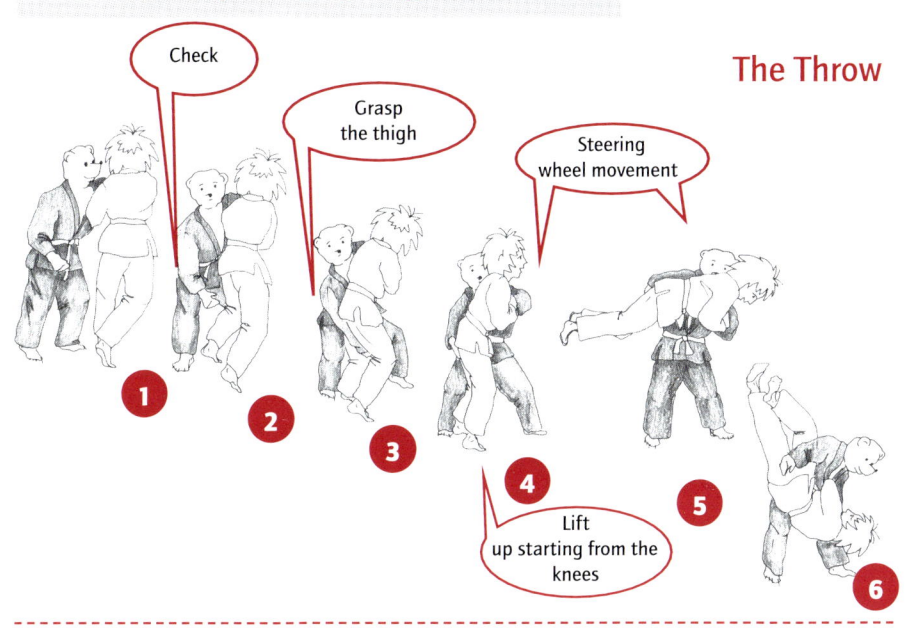

- Check
- Grasp the thigh
- Steering wheel movement
- Lift up starting from the knees

1 — 2 — 3 — 4 — 5 — 6

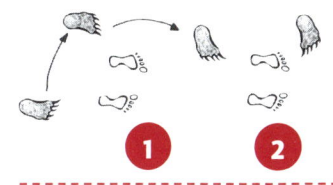

He turns to do a SEOI NAGE throw. With skill you grab his leg and thigh. Now lift him up from knees you grow. Throw him with twist that he will fly on to the mat right down below.

READING NOTES:

Starting position: Your partner is turning to do a SEOI NAGE for example. You check him with your right hand by grasping his leg by the thigh from behind through the legs.

You lift him up starting from down in your knees and tip him over with a steering wheel movement in front of you.

121

5.7 Blue Belt

TE GURUMA (As a counter) (Hand Wheel)

Exercise 1
Look at pictures **1** and **2**: Which throws are illustrated in each picture? Describe the similarities and differences.

_____
_____
_____

Exercise 2
Besides the TE GURUMA, as a counter against the SEOI NAGE, you have already learned other counter techniques. One of these is shown in the picture alongside. Which one is it and against which throws can you use it?

_____
_____
_____
_____

Exercise 3
When you do a TE GURUMA, which parts of the body do the most work?

_____
_____
_____
_____

Exercise 4
Your vocabulary exercise: What do SEOI, TANI, NAGE and KOSHI mean?

TANI = _____   SEOI = _____
NAGE = _____   KOSHI = _____

5.7 Blue Belt
THE FORMS OF JUDO EXERCISES

Has it happened to you sometime or other? The instructor suddenly says, "Alright, now let's have a UKEMI." Everyone stands there, rooted to the spot, and no one wants to take the lead. Also, no one wants to admit that they haven't understood the order. Now you stand there as a candidate for the blue belt and have to demonstrate the movement, while everyone else looks on apprehensively that you are taking the initiative – but only if you knew HOW!! Embarrassing – eh? If only you had paid attention to all those confusing technical terms that abound....

But, at the same time, it's not all that difficult. "UKEMI" for example is all those well known breakfall techniques that you have learned in the meanwhile, nothing further. On the other hand there is a lot more gobbledegook that one needs to use in order to make yourself understood. "TANDOKU RENSHU" means exercising without a partner – sequences of movements and starting postures, for example like you find at the beginning of this book. "UCHI KOMI", on the other hand, are instances where you turn into a throw from a set situation with your partner, and which you will have discussed with him beforehand. Otherwise how can you learn a technique well if your partner is always defending himself? In the "NAGE KOMI" you throw your partner in addition to the movement. "YAKOSOKU GEIKO" serve the same purpose – throws from free movement. Then there is "RANDORI" – well, of course you know all about that in the meanwhile, don't you? That's right; it's the exercise where you have a scrap according to the rules of Judo, and with different partners all the time. And of course you know what the term "SHIAI" means, don't you? The competition – of course! (Come on, did you have to think long about your answer?) And here you will have noted which "NAGE-WAZA" (Throwing techniques) and "NE WAZA" (Groundwork techniques) work well and which ones you still need to practice hard at in the Randori. And again you will know whether your "KUMI KATA" (grips) and "KUZUSHI" (Breaking the balance, pulling movements) still show weak points.....

So – for practice, cover the top half of this page (and don't cheat) and try to remember some things. What was it about:

UCHI KOMI _____	NAGE-WAZA _____
SHIAI _____	KUMI KATA _____
RANDORI _____	TANDOKU RENSHU _____
UKEMI _____	NE-WAZA _____
YAKOSOKU GEIKO _____	KUZUSHI _____
NAGE KOMI _____	

5.8 Brown Belt

ASHI GURUMA (Leg Wheel)

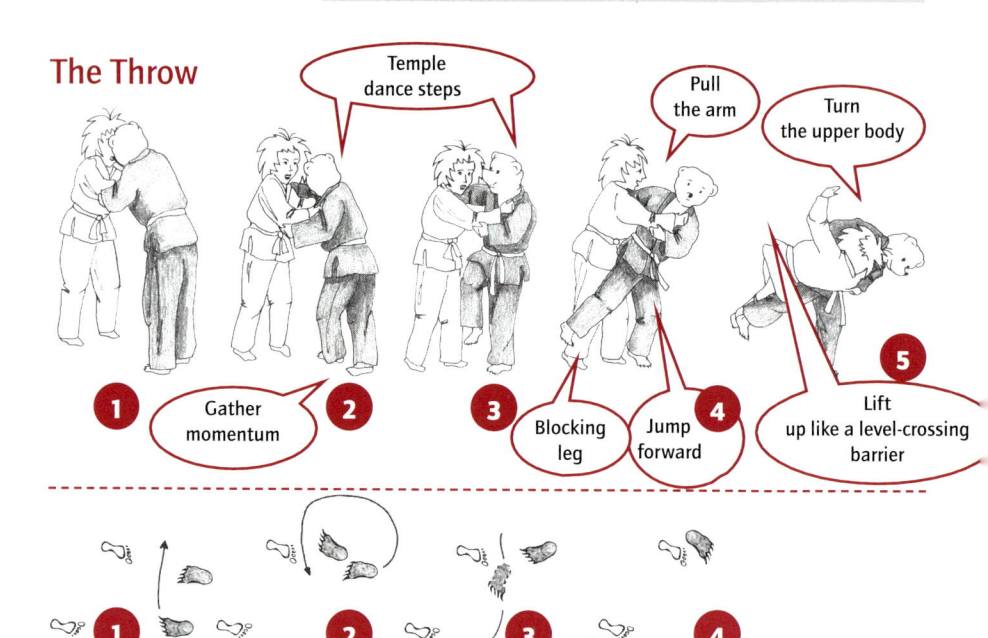

The Throw

1. Gather momentum
2. Temple dance steps
3. Blocking leg
4. Jump forward / Pull the arm
5. Lift up like a level-crossing barrier / Turn the upper body

READING NOTES:

For this throw you need to build up a lot of momentum. Therefore you can throw from a circular movement or by using a KAWAISHI sequence. Here we will start with a right-handed grip. To start the KAWAISHI, place your left foot sideways and forwards in a leg cross-over movement, so that your toes are pointing at your partner, and so that you can build up tension in your hips. (Temple dancer steps). Pull your right foot back in a wide circular movement to gather momentum, so that you can jump with your standing leg right up to him and turn in. Your standing leg lands by the side of your partner. Don't forget to pull your arm diagonally forward. The leg you swing with stays stretched-out as a block to your partner's leg. Your upper body now bends sideways. You throw him with a forceful pull of your arm and a twist of your upper body over the leg acting like a barrier on a level-crossing.

With large temple dancer steps and gait. You gain momentum and jump sideways up to him. Your blocking leg you hold out straight, and over it he tumbles with a din.

5.8 Brown Belt

ASHI GURUMA (Leg Wheel)

Exercise 1
You have learned the KAWAISHI sequence recently. Which other sequences are there? Briefly describe them.

_____
_____
_____
_____
_____

Exercise 2
Which techniques do you know besides, in which the word GURUMA appears? What do all these techniques have in common?

_____
_____
_____
_____

Exercise 3
Which throws are being depicted in pictures **1** and **2** opposite? Briefly describe the details, which are similar and what the differences are.

_____
_____
_____

Exercise 4
Your vocabulary exercise: What do the following words mean?

BARAI   = _____   GARI = _____
HARAI   = _____   GAKE = _____
GAESHI = _____   SASAE = _____

125

5.8 Brown Belt

O GURUMA (Big Wheel)

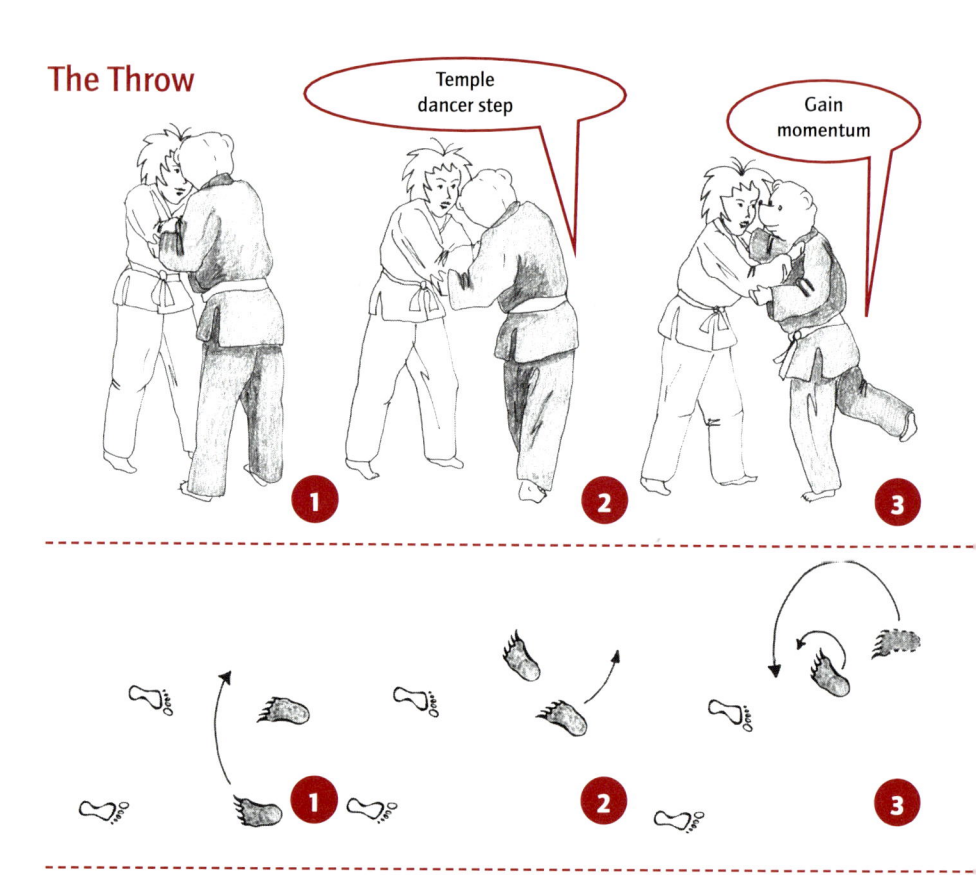

The Throw

Speech bubbles:
1. Temple dancer step
2. Gain momentum

READING NOTES:

For this throw you need to build up a lot of momentum. Therefore you can throw from a circular movement or by using a KAWAISHI starting position.

Here we will start with a right-handed grip. To start the KAWAISHI, place your left foot sideways and forwards in a leg cross-over movement, so that your toes are pointing at your partner, and so that you can build up tension in your hips (Temple dancer steps).

Side note: With temple dancers step and gait, pivot into their partner straight: Your pull becomes his carrier your leg a railway-carrier!

5.8 Brown Belt

O GURUMA (Big Wheel)

Pull your right foot back in a wide circular movement to gather momentum, so that you can jump with your standing leg right up to him and turn in. Your standing leg lands by the side of your partner. The leg you swing with is stretched out so that it is placed across your partner's thighs (acting like a barrier on a level-crossing).

You pull your partner into you (making contact with the side of your body). You throw him in the forward axis – head over heels – and you pull him in so that he is close to you and is turned and falls.

5.8 Brown Belt

O GURUMA (Big Wheel)

Exercise 1
Make a comparison between O GURUMA and ASHI UCHI MATA; Which picture illustrates which throw? How is the standing leg placed? What is the function of the moving leg?

_____
_____
_____
_____
_____

Exercise 2
Draw the sequence of steps for the KAWAISHI sequence in the four empty boxes and indicate which is UKE and TORI.

| 1 | 2 | 3 | 4 |

Exercise 3
Try to describe how the O SOTO GURUMA would look like. Think about the O GURUMA and the O SOTO GARI!

_____
_____
_____

Exercise 4
Your vocabulary exercise: What do ASHI, UCHI, SOTO and GURUMA mean?

ASHI = _____   UCHI = _____
SOTO = _____   GURUMA = _____

5.8 Brown Belt

KATA GURUMA (Kneeling) (Shoulder Wheel)

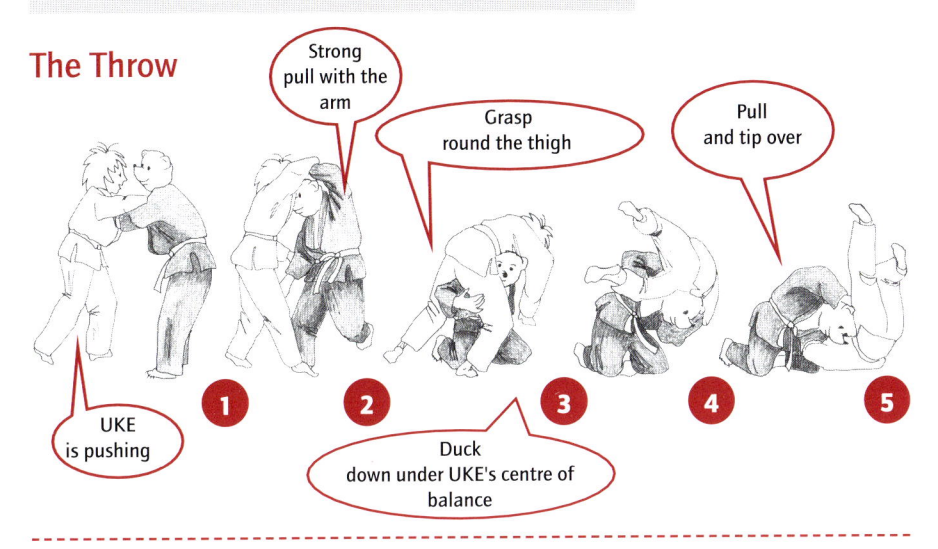

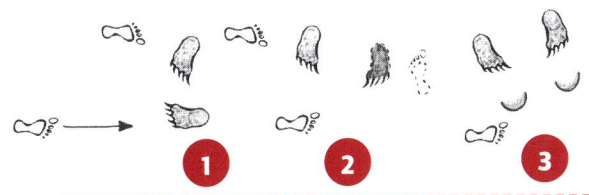

The Throw

- Strong pull with the arm
- Grasp round the thigh
- Pull and tip over
- UKE is pushing
- Duck down under UKE's centre of balance

1 — 2 — 3 — 4 — 5

READING NOTES:

UKE is pushing, and you pull like hell, down on your knees you sink as well. Now with his thigh firmly grasped, you tip him over really fast.

Starting position: Your partner is pushing. You turn your right foot inwards as in the PULLING OUT sequence and pull your partner at the same time sharply forwards, so that he has to take a step forward with his right foot.

While you keep pulling the arm, you drop down onto your knees and grasp from inside around his thigh, so that your neck makes contact with his thigh. With your left hand, pull again, while your right hand lifts him and tips him over and forwards.

5.8 Brown Belt

KATA GURUMA (Shoulder Wheel)

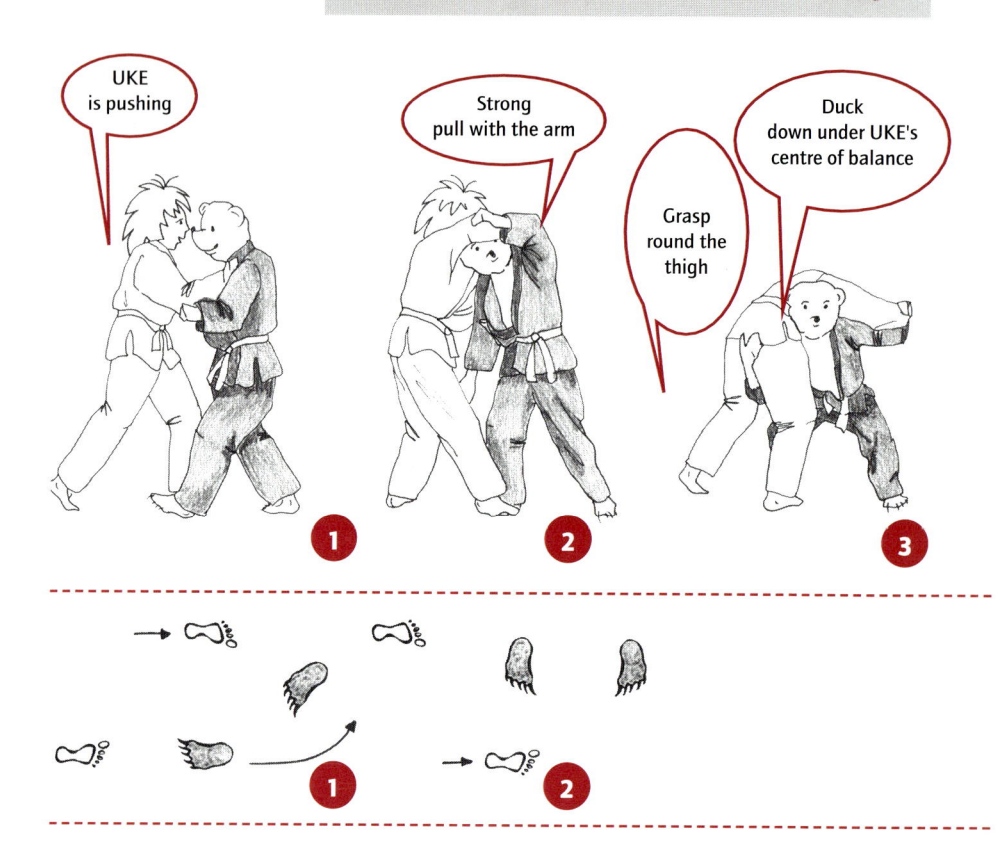

1 UKE is pushing

2 Strong pull with the arm

3 Duck down under UKE's centre of balance / Grasp round the thigh

UKE is pushing, and you pull like hell,
down in your knees you sink as well,
now with his thigh firmly grasped,
stand upright, now the die is cast.

5.8 Brown Belt

KATA GURUMA (Shoulder Wheel)

The Throw

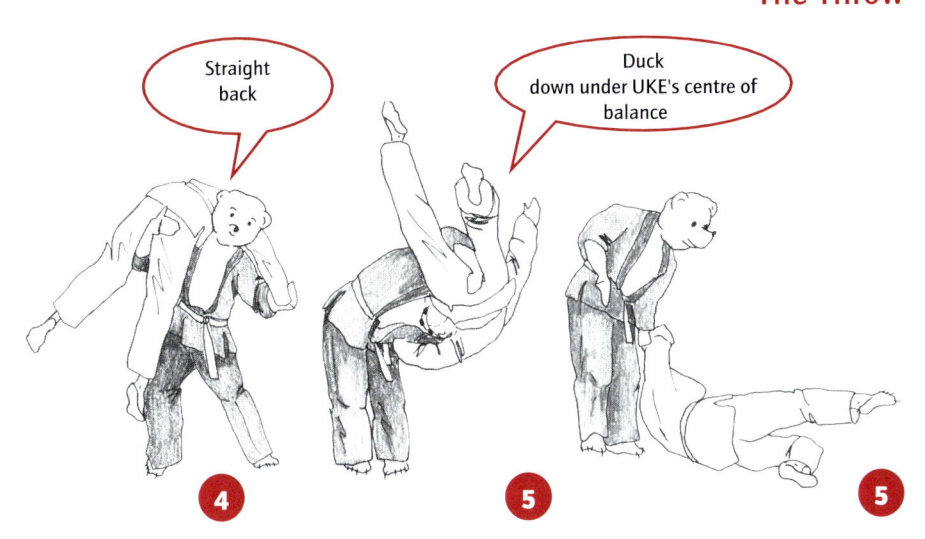

Straight back

Duck down under UKE's centre of balance

4 **5** **5**

READING NOTES:

Starting position: Your partner is pushing. You turn your right foot inwards as in the PULLING OUT starting position and pull your partner at the same time sharply forwards, so that he has to take a step forward with his right foot.

While you keep pulling the arm, you drop down bending your knees and grasp from inside around his thigh, so that your neck makes contact with his thigh. With your left hand, pull again, while your right hand lifts up. You lift him and straighten your back (upright!) and tip him over and forwards.

5.8 Brown Belt

KATA GURUMA
(Shoulder Wheel Kneeling)

Exercise 1
The picture alongside shows the second phase of the KATA GURUMA. Briefly describe the movements that your arms have to carry out.

_____
_____
_____

Exercise 2
Just imagine you do a KATA GURUMA on the knees, but that you turn further round so that you end up with your back to your partner. Where does your arm grasp for the best effect and what throw will evolve from the one, which you would have thrown from a standing position up to now?

_____
_____
_____
_____

Exercise 3
You do a KATA GURUMA throw (see picture). Your partner reacts at this very moment by going hard backwards. What possibilities are open to you?

_____
_____
_____

Exercise 4
Your vocabulary exercise: What do the following words mean?

KATA = _____   SEOI = _____
TE   = _____   HARA = _____

5.8 Brown Belt

KATA GURUMA
(Shoulder Wheel)

Exercise 1
Make a comparison between TE GURUMA and KATA GURUMA; Which picture illustrates which throw? Describe the similarities and differences.

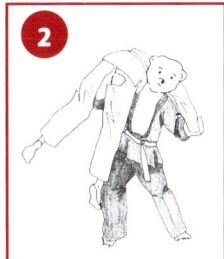

_____
_____
_____

Exercise 2
Why is it so important to keep a straight, upright back when doing the KATA GURUMA?

_____
_____
_____
_____

Exercise 3
Which phase of the throw is depicted in the picture alongside? Describe the most important details, which you must watch out for in this throw?

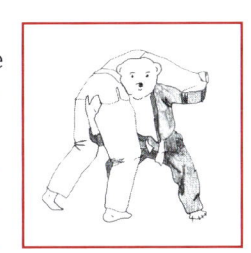

_____
_____
_____

Exercise 4
Your vocabulary exercise: What do the following words mean?

YOKO = _____   MATA = _____
KO = _____   MAKE KOMI = _____

133

5.8 Brown Belt

SOTO MAKI KOMI
(Outer Wraparound Throw)

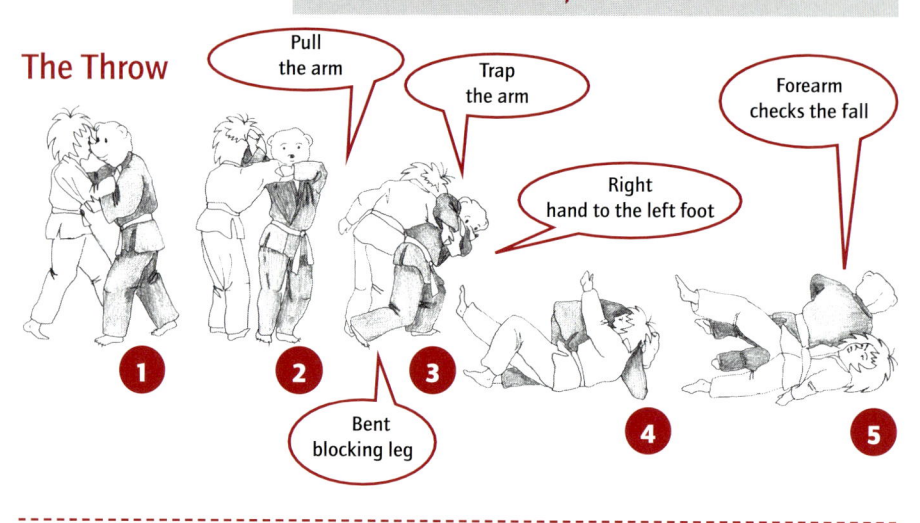

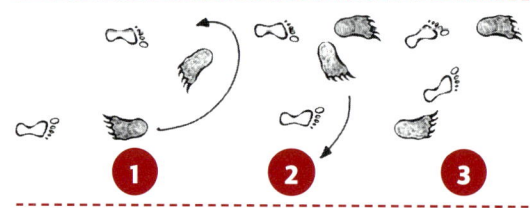

The Throw

1. Pull the arm
2. Trap the arm — Bent blocking leg
3. Right hand to the left foot
4.
5. Forearm checks the fall

READING NOTES:

Pull your partner in with pep, his upper arm now swiftly trap, block him with "TAI-OTHOSHI" step, and land on top the falling chap.

Starting position: Own rearward movement and right-handed grip. You pull your partner hard towards you (look at your watch). At the same time you grasp with your right arm over your partner's right upper arm and trap it under the shoulder. You place your blocking leg on the outside close in front of his legs and drop down deep in your knees (as in the TAI OTOSHI).

While continuing to pull with your arm, you move your right hand towards your left foot. Your forearm checks your fall so that you don't land on your partner's shoulders.

5.8 Brown Belt

SOTO MAKI KOMI
(Outer Wraparound Throw)

Exercise 1
What do your arms do when you do a SOTO MAKI KOMI?
___
___
___
___

Exercise 2
Which throws are illustrated in the two pictures? Make a comparison of their similarities and differences.
___
___
___

Exercise 3
Pictures 1 and 2 show which throws? Briefly describe the individual similarities and differences.
___
___
___

Exercise 4
Your vocabulary exercise: What do the following words mean?

OTOSHI = _____   SOTO = _____
KO   = _____   UCHI = _____

135

5.8 Brown Belt

URA NAGE (Back Throw)

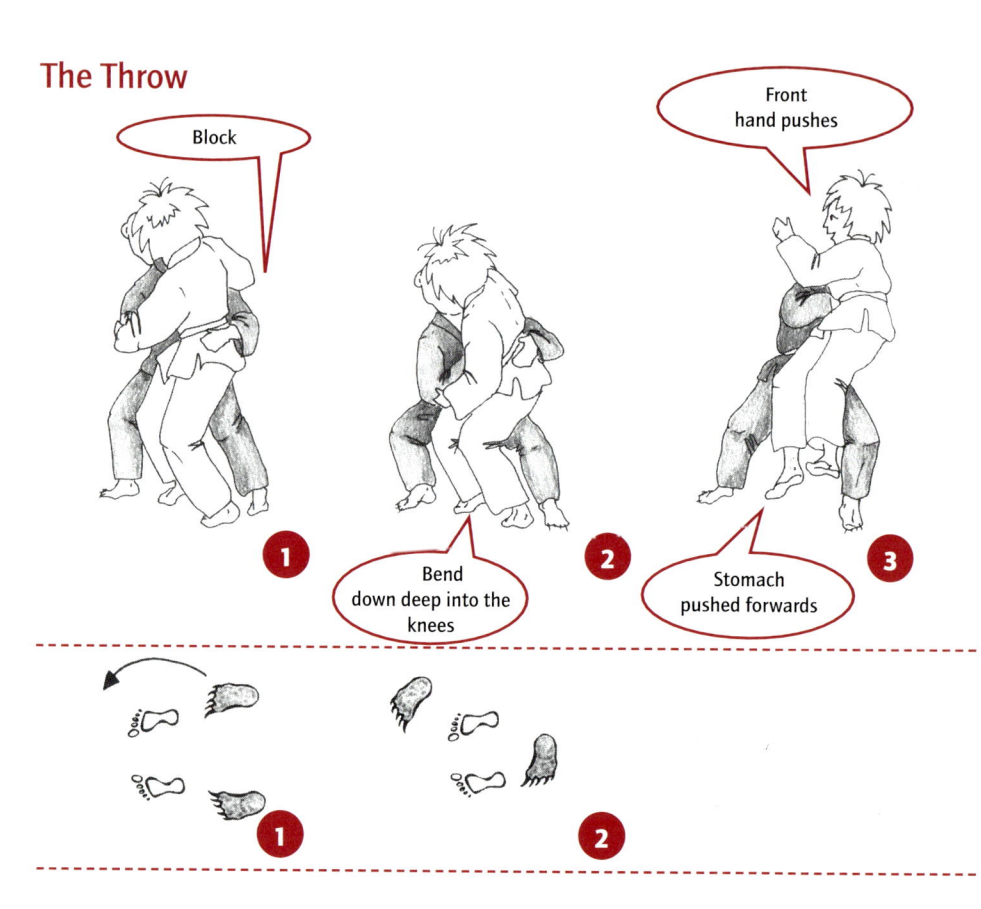

The Throw

Block

Front hand pushes

1

Bend down deep into the knees

2

Stomach pushed forwards

3

1

2

Block and go deep down like lead.
Lift up clear from off the mat,
Tummy pushed forward, turn the head,
and over he goes just like that.

5.8 Brown Belt

URA NAGE (Back Throw)

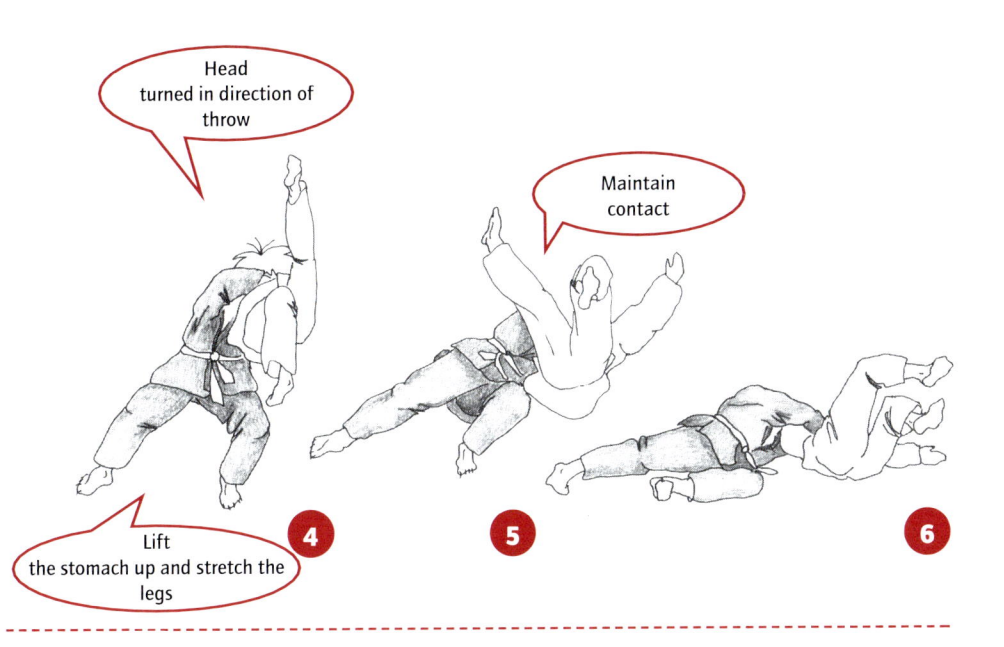

Head turned in direction of throw

Maintain contact

Lift the stomach up and stretch the legs

4 **5** **6**

Tip:
Practice this throw on the soft mat!

READING NOTES:

Your partner is turning to do a hip throw. You step round him and go deep down into the knees, at the same time pushing your left hip forwards (blocking movement). Your left arm grasps firmly round his hips and pulls him in hard. Your right hand is placed firmly against his stomach. Lift him with a rapid, explosive movement, starting from your knees and bringing your stomach forwards. Pull him closer to you and push him backwards with your front hand, pressing your head against his shoulder. Your upper body follows with a twist so that you fall on your side yourself.

5.8 Brown Belt

URA NAGE (Back Throw)

Exercise 1
The URA NAGE can be used as a counter-attack technique against the hip throw. What hip throws do you know up till now?

_____
_____
_____

Exercise 2
Why do you have to step round your partner before you move into an URA NAGE? What happens if you don't step round?

_____
_____
_____
_____

Exercise 3
Why do you have to press your head in and turn your upper body when doing the URA NAGE? What happens if you forget to do this?

_____
_____
_____
_____

Exercise 4
Your vocabulary exercise: What do ASHI, URA, SOTO and NAGE mean?

ASHI = _____   URA = _____
SOTO = _____   NAGE = _____

5.8 Brown Belt

YOKO GURUMA (Side Wheel)

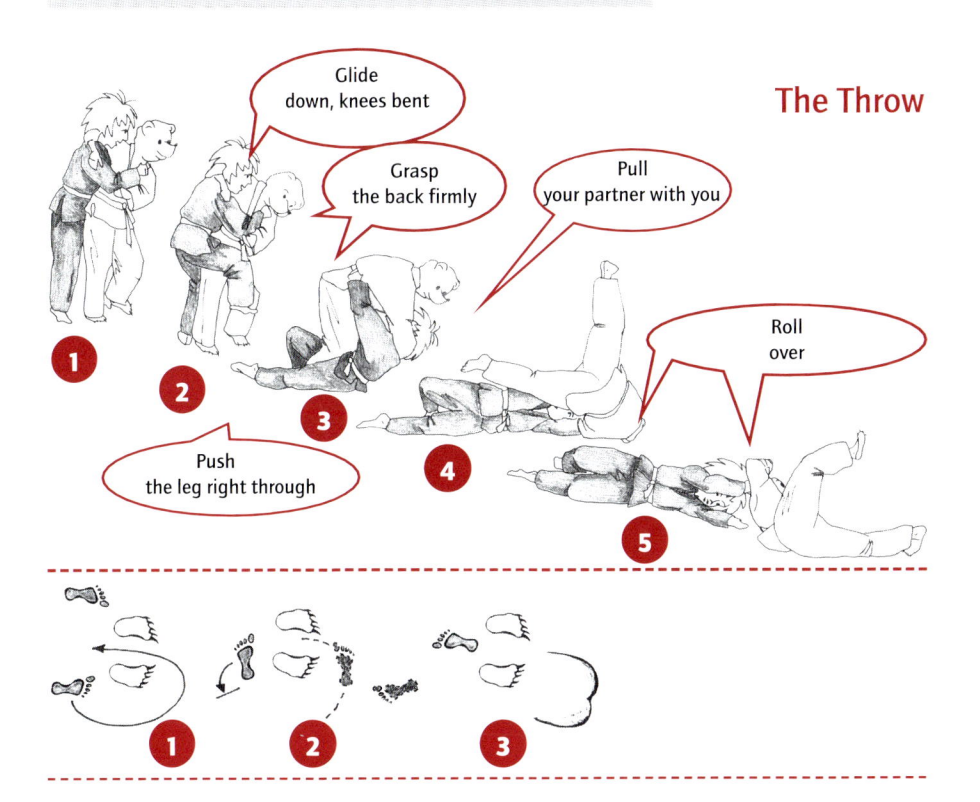

The Throw

(1)
(2) Glide down, knees bent
(3) Grasp the back firmly
Push the leg right through
(4) Pull your partner with you
(5) Roll over

READING NOTES:

Your partner is turning to do a hip throw. He is standing a little bent over so that you can't counter from behind (URA NAGE or TANI OTOSHI). You use this momentum to glide down into a knees bend by his side. Your arm grasps firmly round his hips and you slip your leg between his legs, closing hard up to him. With your other leg stretched out, you block his feet, while at the same time you pull him down using your weight and a strong pull of the arm on his back. You force him to roll over and you follow through.

He pivots in, you glide around, sliding swiftly to the ground.
You win the bout, with leg stretched out, make him roll over safe and sound!

5.8 Brown Belt

YOKO GURUMA (Side Wheel)

Exercise 1
When turning in to do a hip technique, your partner is able to follow various options. Briefly describe what you then have to do. Follow the arrows.

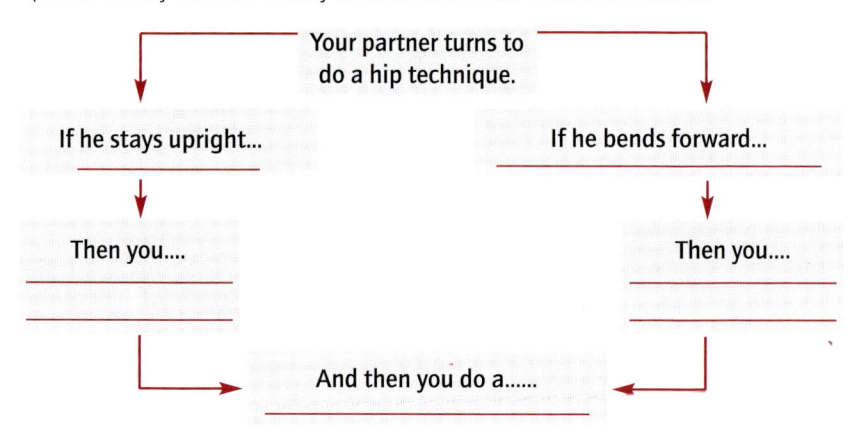

```
                 Your partner turns to
                 do a hip technique.
        ↓                                    ↓
If he stays upright...                If he bends forward...
_____                        _____
        ↓                                    ↓
    Then you....                         Then you....
_____                        _____
_____                        _____
        └──────────→  And then you do a...... ←──────────┘
                      _____
```

Exercise 2
Look at pictures 1 and 2: Which throws are illustrated in each picture? Briefly describe the similarities and differences.

Exercise 3
Your vocabulary exercise: What do the following words mean?

YOKO = _____   NAGE = _____
ASHI = _____   DORI = _____

5.8 Brown Belt

YOUR PROSPECTS

It's almost like a congratulation – after a good test for the "sacred brown", you're moving down the road towards the target you've set yourself. Of course, you would like to reach the DAN or the master grade with the black belt sometime in the distant future. Up until then you will only need just to glance at this book every now and again. But then it's always the same with plans and targets, isn't it? No sooner than you've reached a set target, you ask yourself "What next?" You've nearly finished the pages of this book and already you know a lot about judo.

What can you now get on with?

Perhaps you are a competitor. Then you won't be asking this question at all. You know how many techniques you still have to personally work on in order, either way, to have a small chance of success when putting them into action. You know where the series of movements you do are still a little fluffy at the edges, and that you still have to put in many more hours of training and shed much sweat to achieve a polished result. You must always allow for creativity to emerge in order to improve and develop your techniques into flowing actions – and the measure of your success is after all your success in competition. There is a lot to get through!

It is, however, possible that the contest is not your "thing", even though the variety of judo sporting techniques and their combination options fascinate you. Judo keeps you fit and is fun. In any case, this sport has probably become a sort of 'way of life' for you, and even part of your personality.

You would like to find out more about further techniques and the options for their combination. It interests you to perfect the flowing, harmonious sequences of movements together with your partner, without always having to be measured by your performance in a contest. Perhaps you are interested in having a 'go' at taking part in KATA Championships, where exactly these things are presented in their absolute form by, amongst others, rehearsed teams of partners.

It is also possible that you belong to those who take pleasure in passing on your knowledge to others. Perhaps you have already acted as an assistant during a lesson of instruction. You may have played, secretly, with the thought of becoming yourself an instructor one day, because it would give you pleasure to pass on the specialities of Judo to children or grown-ups. You would want to intensify your own

5.8 Brown Belt

YOUR PROSPECTS

training, both so that you would be able to demonstrate the necessary techniques for a good sequence of movements, and so that you would be able to gain the necessary qualifications to be able to instruct.

Whichever path is the one for you, you should speak about your plans to your friends and, of course, your home trainer. The latter will be able to show you how to realise what you have in mind, and what further training will serve your purpose. In addition, try to make contact with the authorities at regional or national level or take part in courses of instruction on offer in order to train further. There you will certainly come across many more different versions of the techniques that you already know. Stay open-minded about further versions, so that, in the course of time, you will be able to adopt those techniques, that are best for you, into your own style. We wish you much success as you go on your way.....

The Pixie and The Bear

Make a note here – being honest with yourself – what your further aims are and now you will achieve them:

_____

_____

_____

_____

_____

_____

_____

5.9 More Throws

TSUBAME GAESHI
(Swallow Counter)

The Throw

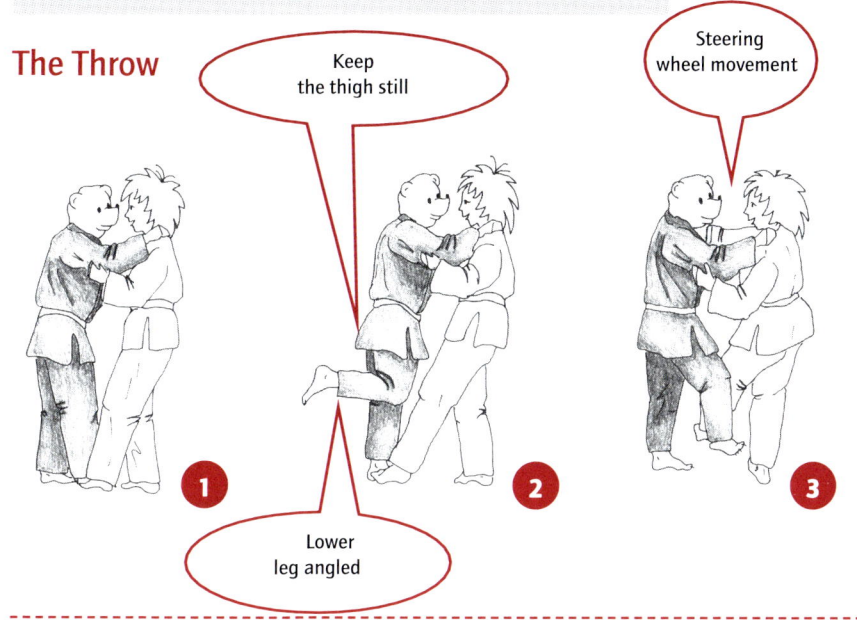

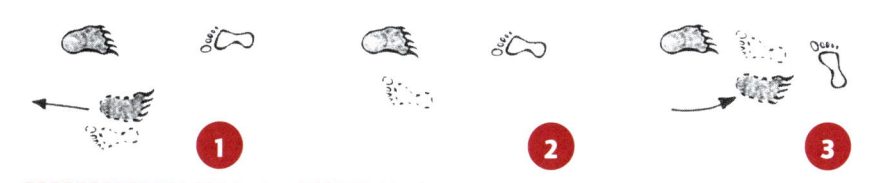

- Keep the thigh still
- Steering wheel movement
- Lower leg angled

1 2 3

1 2 3

READING NOTES:

Your partner is turning to do a DE ASHI BARAI throw. You dodge this. Withdraw your foot swiftly by bending your knee (Note: the thigh is kept still). Now you carry out a DE ASHI BARAI from the outside over his stretched-out foot. Your arms do a steering wheel movement at the same time.

Withdraw your foot: Just bend your knee, sweep him for good, he cannot flee!

Note:
You can also sweep both legs away.

143

5.9 More Throws

TSUBAME GAESHI
(Swallow Counter)

Exercise 1
Describe the movements of how you dodge with your foot and draw them in the three empty boxes below.

| 1 | 2 | 3 |

Exercise 2
Your partner starts to do a SASAE TSURI KOMI ASHI. Describe how you can dodge this so that you can follow through and throw your partner. Which throw can you use for this?

_____
_____
_____
_____
_____
_____
_____
_____

Exercise 3
Your vocabulary exercise: What do the following words mean?

GAESHI   = _____

SUMI   = _____

TSUBAME = _____

144

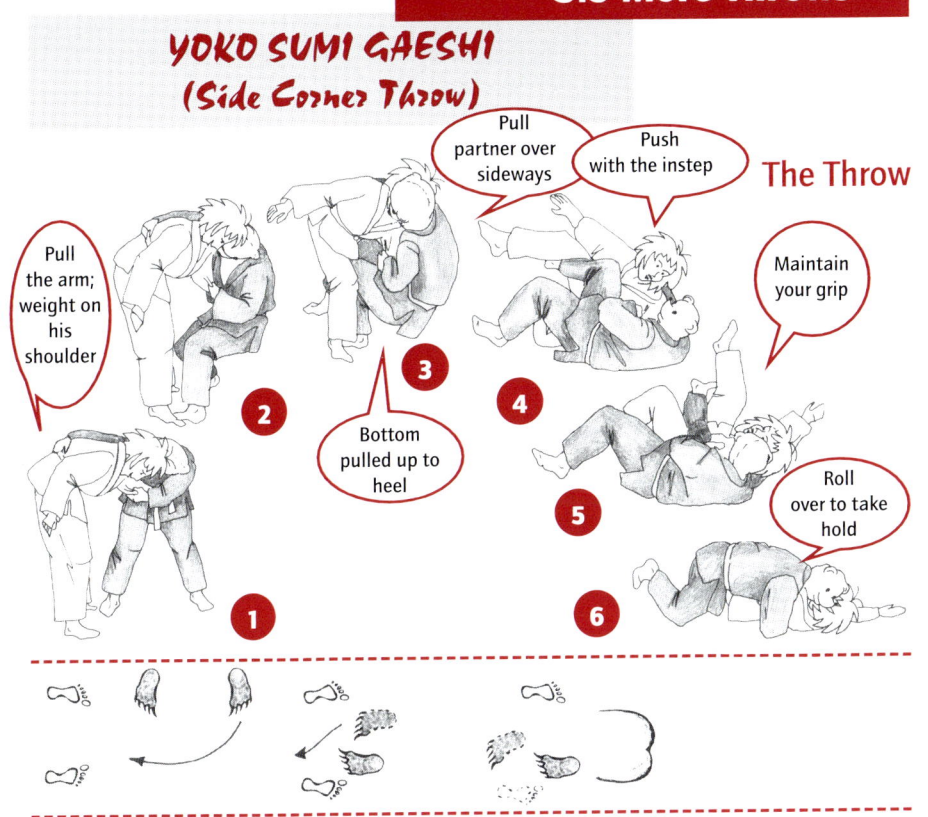

5.9 More Throws

YOKO SUMI GAESHI
(Side Corner Throw)

The Throw

- Pull the arm; weight on his shoulder
- Pull partner over sideways
- Push with the instep
- Maintain your grip
- Bottom pulled up to heel
- Roll over to take hold

1 — 2 — 3 — 4 — 5 — 6

If UKE's slightly forwards bent, you smilingly support this trend, weight on his shoulder, grip his back, his arm across your stomach drag, slip in your bottom to your heels and pull him sideways til he reels, push with your instep (that´s my tip), roll over and maintain your grip.

READING NOTES:

Starting situation: You stand opposite each other with feet positioned in a "V". Your partner is bending over slightly. You grasp his diagonal arm and pull him close across your body. With the other hand you grab him far down his back and pull him close in (pull the arm in and place weight on his shoulder). Step forward with your left leg in front of his feet. You slip your bottom right up to your heel. At the same time you pull his arm further across your stomach and pull your partner down sideways using the grip on his back. You support his sideways tipping by pushing round his thigh with the instep of your leading leg. Maintain your grip until he is lying on the ground, so that you can roll over to follow through with a holding grip.

5.9 More Throws

KHABARELLI
(Named after a Georgian Judoka)

The Thrown

Grasp the belt; keep close contact

Straight back

Grip on the material below the knee

Lift up from the knees

1 **2** **3**

1 **2** **3**

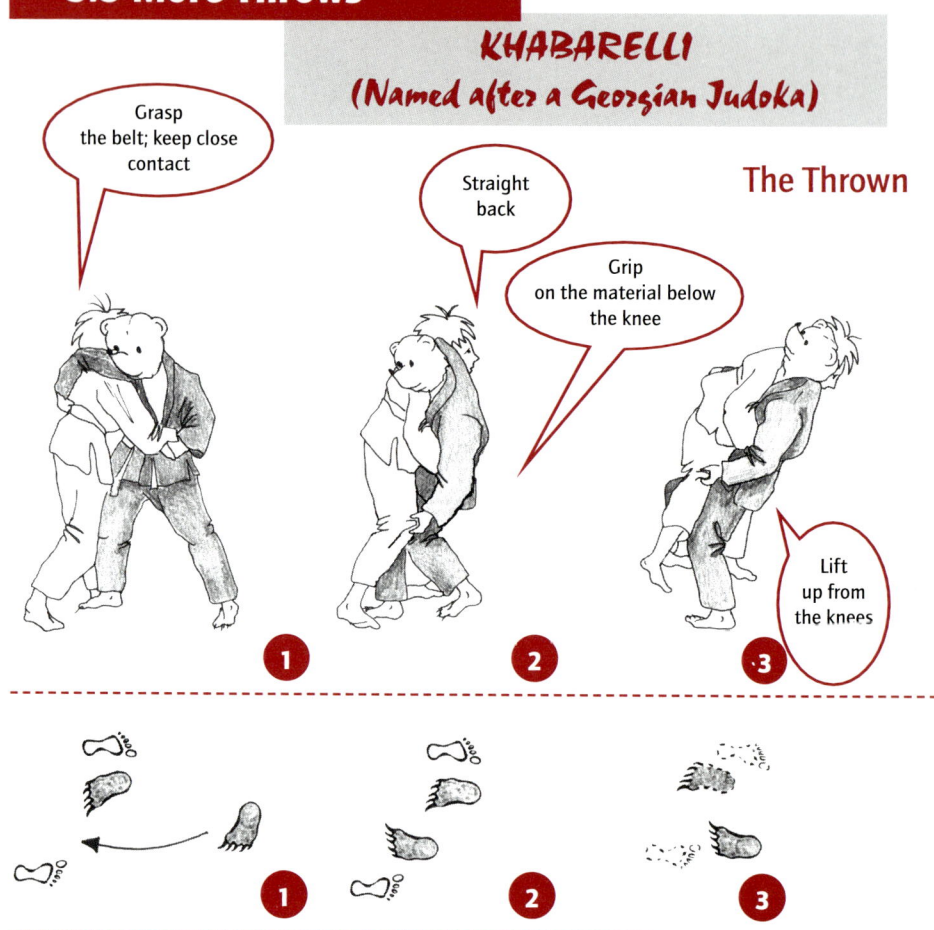

READING NOTES:

Your partner is standing a little bent over. You have grasped him by the arm and you pull it diagonally in front of you. Your other arm grips his belt and your armpit is close to his shoulder.

You pull your rear leg forward so that your hips are below your partner's centre of balance. Your hand lets his arm go free and grasps the material of his suit just below the knee.

You lift him up, starting from the knees, using both arms. Your right leg supports the movement by bringing it up and outwards.

5.9 More Throws

KHABARELLI
(Named after a Georgian Judoka)

Balloon callouts on figures 4, 5, 6:
- Lift leg upwards and outwards
- Balanced backwards
- Look in direction of throw

4   **5**   **6**

> Grap happily over his shoulder,
> and below his knee (ere he gets older).
> Now you give him a lift,
> turning backwards and shift
> him around so he falls like a boulder.

You bring your hips forwards and tilt your head and upper body backwards until you come to a backwards balanced position (the other way round than in the UCHI MATA). By turning your upper body and using your arms you throw him over.

Tip:
It is recommended, and not at all a weak point, to practice this throw on the soft mat.

5.9 More Throws

YOKO SUMI GAESHI
(Side Corner Throw)

Exercise 1
Describe the movement your arms do in the YOKO SUMI GAESHI.

_____
_____
_____
_____

Exercise 2
Which throws are illustrated in pictures 1 and 2? Briefly describe the similarities and differences.

_____
_____
_____

Exercise 3
Describe as follows: How could you combine the ASHI UCHI MATA and the YOKO SUMI GAESHI? How would the sequence of movements in the YOKO SUMI GAESHI change as a result?

_____
_____
_____
_____

Exercise 4
Your vocabulary exercise: What do the following words mean?

GAESHI = _____   MATA = _____
YOKO   = _____   SUMI = _____

5.9 More Throws

KHABARELLI
(Named after a Georgian Judoka)

Exercise 1
Compare the ASHI UCHI MATA and the KHABARELLI. Which picture illustrates which of the throws? What are the similarities and differences.

_____
_____
_____

Exercise 2
Which other techniques can be combined into the KHABARELLI? What movements will your partner have to make for this?

_____
_____
_____
_____

Exercise 3
What options do you have to develop the necessary grip holds that are required in the KHARABELLI? What other techniques can you start from the same grip holds?

_____
_____
_____
_____

Exercise 4
Your vocabulary exercise: What do the following words mean?

TSURI = _____   GAESHI = _____
O = _____   SASAE = _____

149

5.9 More Throws

KOGA SEOI NAGE

The Throw

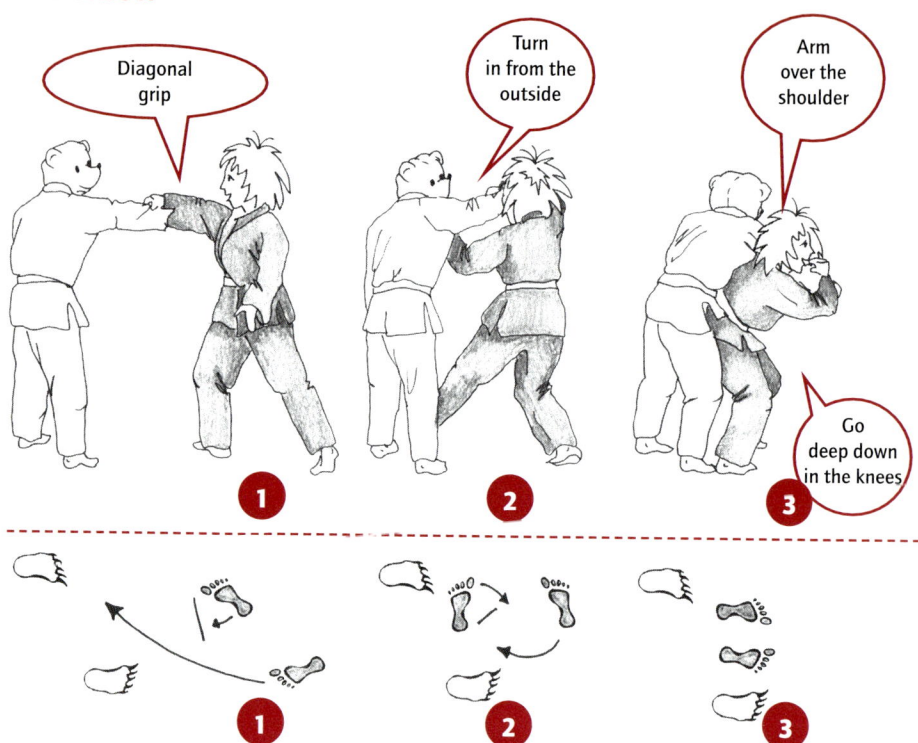

1. Diagonal grip
2. Turn in from the outside
3. Arm over the shoulder / Go deep down in the knees

Grip his arm and pull him wide,
and pivot in far from outside.
Keep your knees bent deep,
then come up and quite steep
from your shoulder he'll certainly slide.

5.9 More Throws

(Koga – Shoulder Throw – Named after a Japanese Judoka)

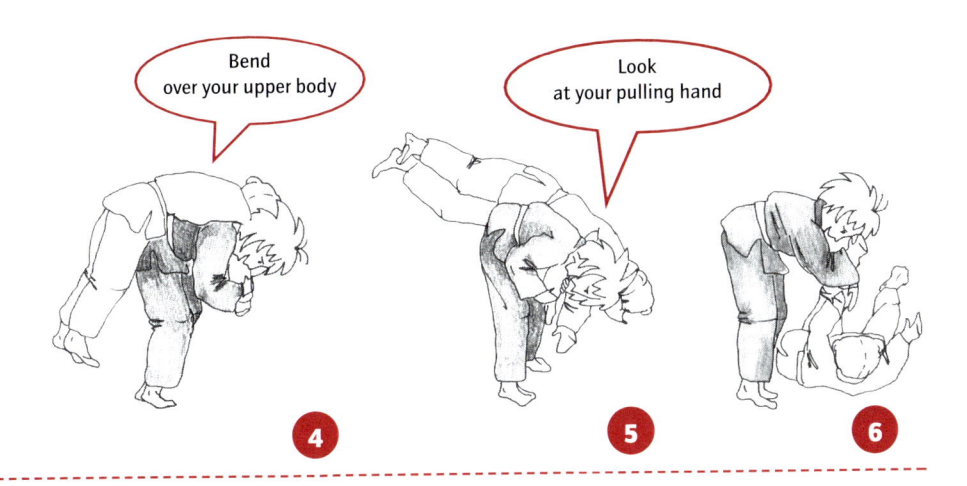

Bend over your upper body

Look at your pulling hand

4 **5** **6**

READING NOTES:

You grasp your partner's arm with a diagonal hold. From the outside, you turn left into an IPPON SEOI NAGE by taking a firm step in front of your partner's legs and at the same time pulling his right arm over your left shoulder.

You step back round in a half-circle and at the same time go down to a knees bend.

Continue pulling the arm and do the throw over your left shoulder by bending over your upper body, whilst at the same time looking at your pulling hand.

5.9 More Throws

KOGA SEOI NAGE
(Koga – Shoulder Throw)

Exercise 1
Compare the IPPON SEOI NAGE and the KOGA SEOI NAGE: Which picture illustrates which throw? What are the similarities and differences?

_____
_____

Exercise 2
Your partner has grasped you with a lapel hold with his right hand. How can you turn this into a starting situation for the KOGA SEOI NAGE?

_____
_____
_____
_____
_____

Exercise 3
What other forms of the SEOI NAGE do you know?

_____
_____
_____
_____

Exercise 4
Your vocabulary exercise: What do the following words mean?

IPPON = _____   MOROTE = _____
SEOI = _____   SASAE = _____

5.9 More Throws

YOKO GAKE
(Side Body Drop)

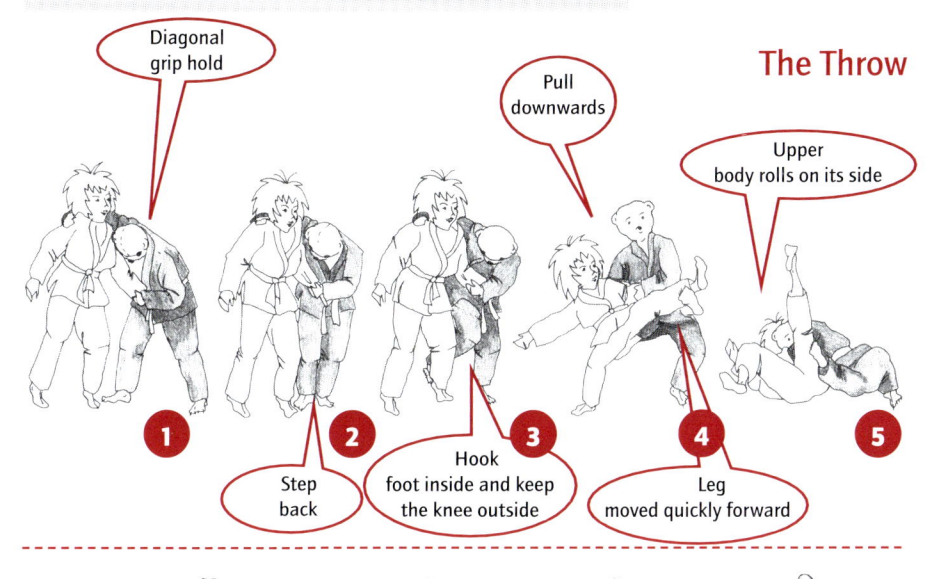

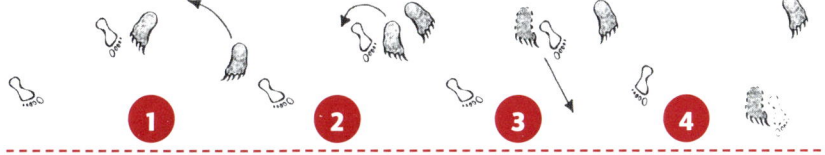

The Throw

- 1. Step back — Diagonal grip hold
- 2. Hook foot inside and keep the knee outside — Pull downwards
- 3.
- 4. Leg moved quickly forward
- 5. Upper body rolls on its side

READING NOTES:

Hook in well, and pull hard back. Your leg shoots forward wide, that will get him on his back. Turn on him from the side!

Starting situation: You stand opposite each other with feet positioned in a "V". Your partner is bending over slightly. You grasp his diagonal arm and pull him close across your body, and at the same time you step backwards. He reacts by going back in order to dodge the ASHI UCHI MATA he has presumed you will attempt. With this movement, you use this opportunity to hook your leg into his weighted leg from behind (foot inside, knee outside). You pull him hard back by his high collar and quickly push your hip and your leg, which is hooked in, forward. Your upper body turns towards him so that you fall on your side.

Note:
It's best to practice this throw on the soft mat!

5.9 More Throws

YOKO GAKE
(Side Body Drop)

Exercise 1
To which group of throws does the YOKO GAKE belong? The ASHI, KOSHI, TE or SUTEMI WAZA group? Which other throws belong to these groups?

_____
_____
_____
_____
_____
_____

Exercise 2
Briefly describe how your partner reacts when you start an ASHI UCHI MATA and say what you then have to do. Follow the arrows.

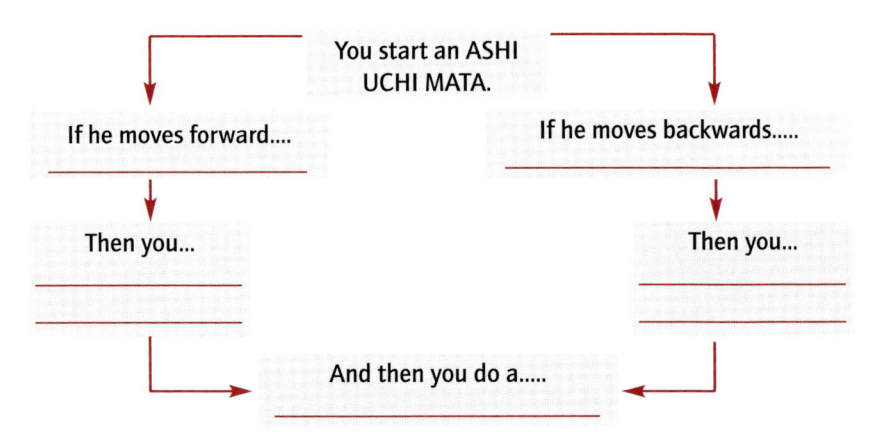

You start an ASHI UCHI MATA.

If he moves forward....
_____

Then you...
_____
_____

If he moves backwards.....
_____

Then you...
_____
_____

And then you do a.....
_____

Exercise 3
Your vocabulary exercise: What do the following words mean?

GAESHI = _____   GAKE = _____
YOKO   = _____   ASHI = _____

6 THE THROWING CIRCLE

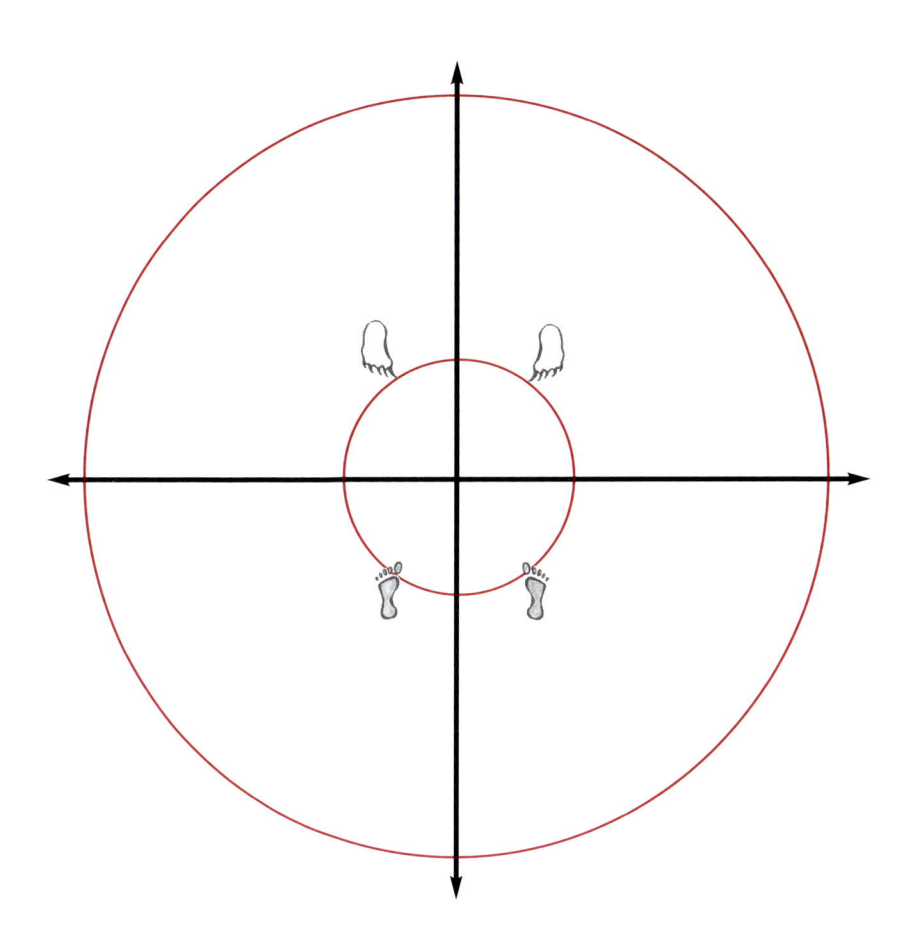

And now you have the chance - after you have learned a lot of new throws from this book – to construct your own throwing circle with all your most favourite throws. Try to cover all possible sectors with your throws and look for the best suitable combinations of throws.

Have fun thinking this out!

155

7 COMPETITION CARD

When you often go to competitions, it's worthwhile to carefully watch and observe opponents, who you regularly 'meet' on the mat, so that you can adjust your tactics and style accordingly. The following competition card example should help you learn what points you should concentrate on.

Name, Christian Name   _____

Grip holds:
(indicate on
the drawing
of the judogi
where he grips)

Right-footed stance   O   Left-footed stance   O

Prefers standing fight O   Prefers groundwork fight   O

Starting techniques: _____
                        _____

Main technique: _____

Follow through technique: _____
                          _____
                          _____

Groundwork techniques: _____
                        _____
                        _____

Specialities: _____
                        _____

8 GLOSSARY

A MINI JAPANESE VOCABULARY

ASHI	Leg, foot
ASHI WAZA	Technique using the leg or foot
BARAI	Sweeping action (usually with the leg)
DORI	Grip
DAN	Master grade (Black belt)
GAESHI	Counter-attack
GAKE	Hook
GARI	to reap
GURUMA	Wheel
HAJIME	"Begin!"
HANE	Springing motion
HANSOKU MAKE	Disqualification
HARA	Stomach, belly
HARAI	Sweeping action, usually with the leg (see also 'Barai' above)
HIDARI	Left
HIZA	Knee
IPPON	Point (highest score in a competition)
KATA	One (once); shoulder
KEIKOKU	Penalty (a waza-ari is awarded to the opponent)
KO	Small
KOKA	Advantage (lowest score in a competition)
KOSHI	Hip
KOSHI WAZA	Technique using the hip
KUCHIKI	Dead tree
KUMI KATA	Gripping methods
KUZUSHI	Breaking the balance
KYU	Beginner's grade

157

A MINI JAPANESE VOCABULARY

MAKI	Rolling down, wrapping
MAKI KOMI	Pinning yourself to your partner and rolling down to the floor
MA SUTEMI WAZA	Straight sacrifice throws
MATA	Thigh
MATTE	"Stop!"
MIGI	Right
MOKUSO	Concentrate (when greeting)
MOROTE	With both hands
NAGE	A throw
NAGE WAZA	Throwing techniques
NE WAZA	Groundwork techniques
O	Large
OKURI	Both
OSAE KOMI	Hold down
OTOSHI	Drop down
RANDORI	Sparring
REI	"Greetings!" (at beginning/a bow)
SASAE	Stopping, halting
SE	Back (part of body)
SEOI	Take up onto your back
SHIAI	Official contest/competition
SHIDO	Penalty (a 'koka' is awarded to the opponent)
SONE MAMA	"Do not move!" (Referee's command)
SORE MADE	"No more!" (End of contest)
SOTO	Outside, outer
SUMI	Corner
SUTEMI	Sacrifice/literally: "to throw away"
TACHI WAZA	Standing techniques
TAI	Body
TANI	Valley

A MINI JAPANESE VOCABULARY

TAOSHI	Press together/round
TE	Hand
TE WAZA	Technique using the hand
TOKETA	"Hold broken!"
TOMOE	Turning over, twisting over
TORI	The person throwing
TSUBAME	Swallow (as in bird)
TSURI	Flicking back action with the wrist/to fish
UCHI	Inner, inside
UCHI KOMI	Sequence/exercise up to the point of throw
UKE	The person being thrown
UKEMI	Breakfall technique
UKI WAZA	Floating throw
URA NAGE	Back throw
USHIRO	Rearwards, backwards
UTSURI	Changing (sides)
WAKI	Side, side of the body
WAZA	Technique
WAZA-ARI	Half-a-point in a competition
WAZA-ARI AWASETE IPPON	2 half points making one point in a competition
YAKOSOKU GEIKO	A series of throws carried out from a free movement
YOKO	Sideways
YOKO SUTEMI WAZA	Sideways sacrifice techniques
YUKO	Medium point score in a competition

A MINI JAPANESE VOCABULARY 2

Here is room for you to write down more Japanese words and terms, which you have learned in training and, which you would like to make a note of:

Sode   **Sleeve**

9 CUT OUT PAGES

For the exercises

O SOTO OTOSHI:

SASAE TSURI KOMI ASHI:

For the exercises

DE ASHI BARAI:

For the exercises

KOSHI GURUMA:

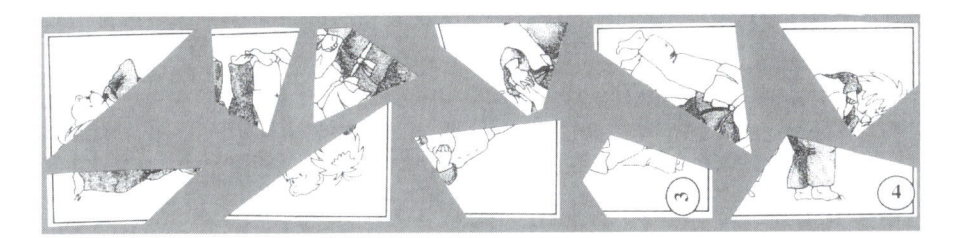

O GOSHI:

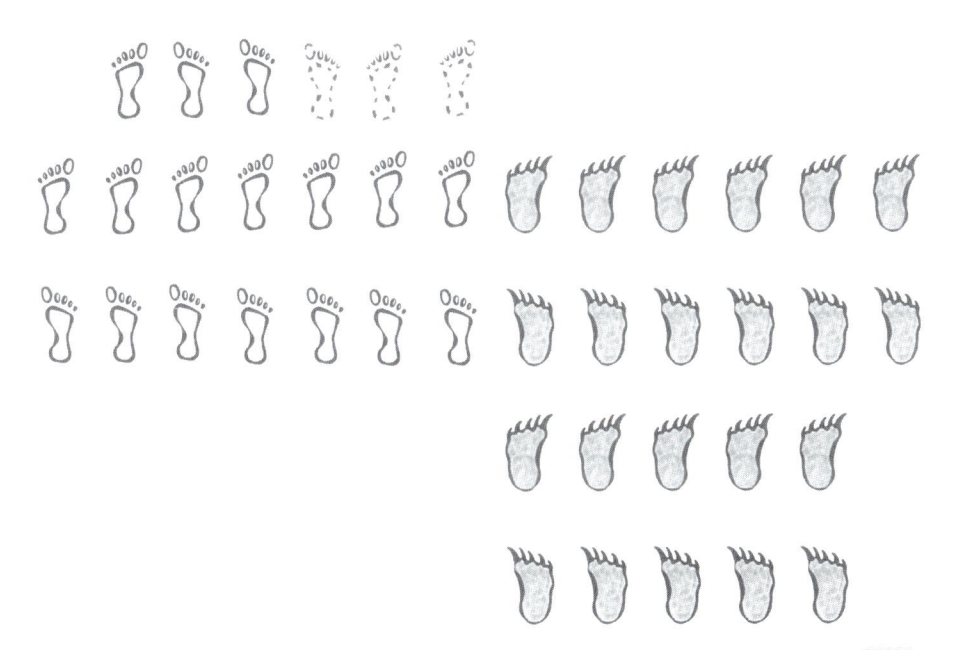

163

For the exercises

O UCHI BARAI:

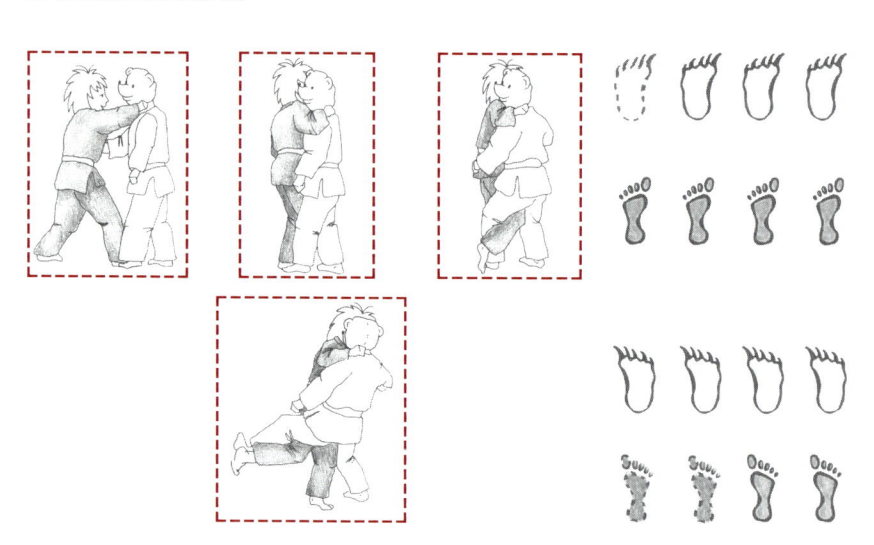

KO UCHI BARAI:

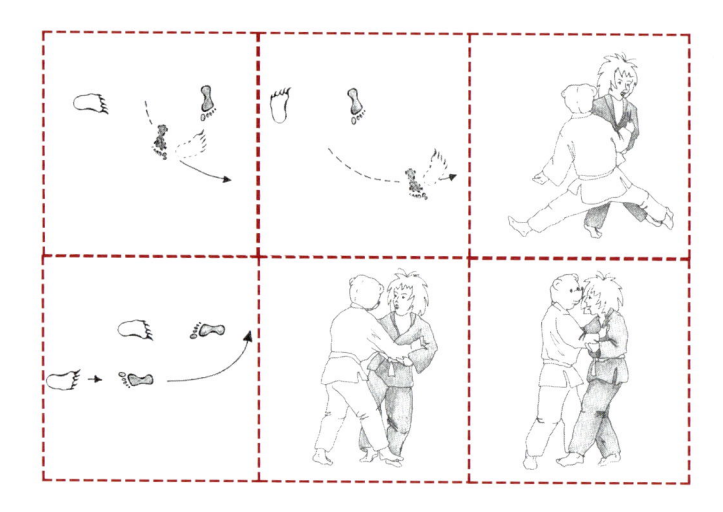

For the exercises

TOMOE NAGE:

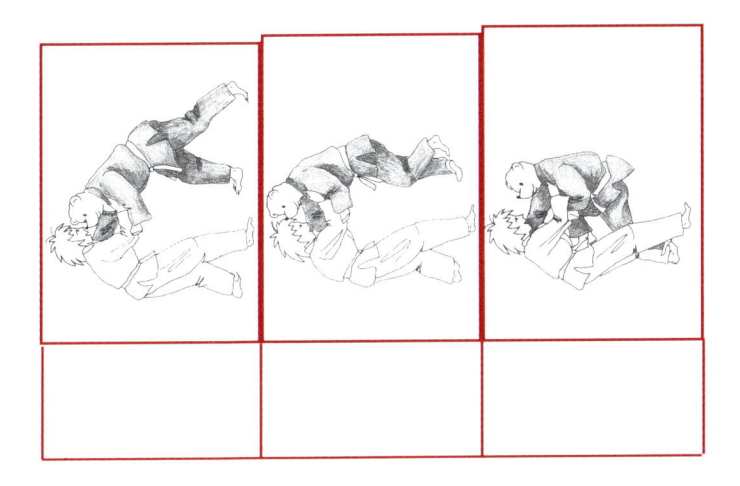

11 Postscript

Well that's it! If you have managed to digest all we have included here and have managed to master somehow all the exercises, then you have notched up quite an advance with your favourite sport.

But just think about it: **No book can replace practice and take away the effort you need to put in, in order to execute a throw well.** You will need a lot of patience and accuracy – even when you do the 195th repeat of a throw – in order to achieve this.

In all ways, we wish you find a good partner and have a lot of fun practising.

Yours,
The little Pixie and the little Bear

By the way:
The little Pixie and the little Bear actually do exist.
Behind the scenes are the couple of people, who have written this book for you:

THE AUTHORS

In real life, the little bear is called **Björn Deling** and looks back at over 20 years experience of Judo. He doesn't look that old though, does he?
He began Judo – like you – as a small child and then later, as an active competitor, he collected bags of experience and realised that he had to train long, hard and exacting in order, for example, to become German Judo Champion. But, then you will already have learned that you have to do all this from reading this book. For several years now he has been passing on his experience in both Competitive and General Sports as a trainer of children. Together with the little pixie he had the idea for this book when they both found they were always being asked by the children what they had to do and learn for the grading tests. So he has put together and written out all that is important for the successful execution of the various different throws.

In real life, the little pixie is called **Dr Hedda Sander**. She has been a trainer for several years and knows through her own three children, who, like you, are Judo fans, how important sketches and illustrations are in understanding the different throws. So, she sat down and thought up the idea for you of a little bear and a little pixie as comic characters, who toddle along and train together in this book.
    Together with the little bear, she has actually had a video film made of her and the little bear as they demonstrated all the throws that you need to learn. From this video film, and after a lot of work, the sketches were made into what you see here for each of the techniques, just like in a cartoon. Making sure that the individual details for the successful execution of each technique were correct was very important to her, so that you could "read" the pictures if you could not get a clear understanding from parts of the text.

At this juncture, the Pixie and the Bear would like, once again, to thank all those who have given their support in both fruitful discussion and patient checking of the texts and contents. In particular, Heiner Sauer has helped enormously with his valuable encouragement. Gottfried Burucker is thanked as well for the careful checking of the sketches. Similarly we would like to thank Hermann Rossberg and the Brunswick Police Force for the generosity of putting the Dojo at our disposal.

APPENDIX

"STARDUST" ANSWERS

Hedda Sander/Björn Deling

STARDUST ANSWERS TO THE PIXIE'S QUESTIONS

Accompanying Appendix

"STARDUST" ANSWERS

General Notes:

Please check the actual notes on the page concerning each action for the foot sequences and throwing sequences. For Japanese terminology, please use the glossary.

Sequences:
Page 27
Ex 1.   UKE pushes strongly: PULLING OUT.
        UKE pulls lightly: KODOKAN forwards.
        TORI right-footed stance: KODOKAN forwards, straight sequence, KAWAISHI.
        UKE pushes lightly: KODOKAN rearwards.
        TORI pulls UKE round in a circle: KODOKAN, KAWAISHI.
        Sideways movement: straight sequence, KODOKAN.
Ex 2.   In order to get under the partner's centre of balance.

Page 29
Ex 4.   A = PULLING OUT
        B = KODOKAN rearwards
        C = KODOKAN forwards
Ex 5.   Phase 3-5 .... the same
        In one you brace your foot down to the rear (B); in the other (C) it's to the fore.

Page 30
Ex 6.   A = UKE pushes strongly.
        B = UKE pushes lightly.
        C = UKE pulls or stands still.
Ex 7.   UKE pushes strongly, therefore use PULLING OUT sequence, otherwise he will run round you. UKE pushes lightly, therefore use KODOKAN rearwards, in order to get under his centre of balance.
Ex 8.   All sequences are possible, choice of sequence depends on your own and UKE's movements.

Throws
Page 32
Ex 1.   Colour in the Bear = TORI
Ex 2.   1 = O GOSHI

"STARDUST" ANSWERS

2 = KOSHI GURUMA
"Elastic knees", Pull the arm
Similarities: Hip throws, elastic knees and pull of the arm are important.
Differences: O GOSHI – grab round the hips.
KOSHI GURUMA – trap the head.

Page 34

Ex 1. Contact shoulder to shoulder, blocking leg outside and forward.

Page 36

Ex 2. Stepping movement backwards, partner pushes,
Side step out of the movement (elastic knees), pull of the arm and push, outstretched leg.

Ex 3. SASAE TSURI KOMI ASHI.

Page 38

Ex 2 Go backwards, wait, stirr and then sweep with the sole of the stretched-out leg against the unweighted leg – just before she sets it down. Steering wheel movement – arm inside.

Page 40

Ex 2 Forwards movement, the forward, less weighted leg is the one that is swept away. The DE ASHI BARAI from a rearwards movement is started by waiting and a slight stirring movement, the rear, unweighted leg is the one that is swept away.

Page 46

Ex 2 Phase 3: High collar grip, pull partner tightly towards you, look at your watch, Charlie Chaplin steps.
Phase 4: Hold wrist straight, elastic knees, head turns with the pull, pull the arm (look at your watch), right foot forward.

Page 49

Ex 2 Lock the arm tightly in crook of the elbow.
Bend your leg round your partner's leg – blocking leg close to your partner and go down low .

Page 51

Ex 1 Partner reacts rearwards: KO UCHI GARI.
Partner reacts forwards: KOSHI GURUMA

Ex 2 1=Phase 1; strong pull with the arm.
2=Phase 3; Reap with the sole of the stretched-out leg, arms are pushed downwards.

"STARDUST" ANSWERS

Page 53
Ex 1 Partner reacts forwards = KOSHI GURUMA
Partner reacts backwards = O UCHI GARI, follow through with a grip hold.
Ex 2 1,3 = O UCHI GARI
2,4 = KO UCHI GARI
Both you and your partner adopt an opposite starting stance
(e.g., TORI a left-footed stance, UKE a right-footed stance)
Both you and your partner adopt the same starting stance
(e.g., both of you start with a right-footed stance) in the KO UCHI GARI.

Page 55
For example SASAE TSURI KOMI ASHI, KOSHI GURUMA.

Page 57
Ex 1 Continually glide down low in the knees in order to get under your partner's centre of balance, when throwing, stretch the leg first of all when you bend over your body.
Ex 2 1 = SEOI OTOSHI
2 = SEOI NAGE
Similarities: Locking the arm
Differences: 1 = Blocking leg close in front of partner's leg while bending the knees.
2 = Drop down low in the knees without using a blocking leg, feet shoulder-width apart.

Page 59
Ex 1 Phase 2: Elbow tucked under the shoulder with a firm wrist.
Ex 2 Right hand = Lifting hand (Elbow tucked under the left shoulder/firm wrist).
Left hand = Pulling hand (look at your watch).
Ex 3 1 = TSURI KOMI GOSHI
2 = IPPON SEOI NAGE
Similarities: Go deep down in the knees under the partner's centre of balance.
Differences: 1 = Elbow tucked under the shoulder with a firm wrist.
2 = Trap the arm and lock in.

Page 61
Ex 1 TSURI KOMI GOSHI

"STARDUST" ANSWERS

	Elbows tucked under the partner's shoulder and press with a firm wrist – this movement is also in the TAI OTOSHI.
Ex 2	1 = TAI OTOSHI
	2 = SEOI OTOSHI
	Similarities: Blocking leg close in front of the partner's leg and go deep down in the knees.
	Differences: 1 = Elbow tucked under the shoulder with a firm wrist.
	2 = Trap the arm and lock in.
Ex 3	1 = TSURI KOMI GOSHI
	2 = TAI OTOSHI
	Similarities: Arm placed under the partner's shoulder, firm wrist, strong pull.
	Differences: 1 = Go down low without using a blocking leg.
	2 = Blocking leg placed close in front of the partner's leg.

Page 63

Ex 1	Forwards (along the centre axis of the feet), where his stance is at weakest You pull in the direction of the knot in the belt (see picture 3 and 4 of the sequence).
Ex 2	1 = TAI OTOSHI (Straight sequence)
	2 = TAI OTOSHI (KODOKAN rearwards)
	Similarities: Arm is pulled in the same direction, elbow is placed under the shoulder.
	Differences: 1 = Cross-over forwards.
	2 = Cross-over to the rear.
Ex 3	Diagonally forwards and diagonally to the rear, partner stands at weakest in the right-footed stance.

Page 65

Ex 1	The Bear = TORI; 4, 1, 3, 2.
Ex 2	Contact (shoulder to shoulder, sweeping through to a balanced one-legged standing position).
Ex 4	Straight arm slaps down on the ground, chin held on the chest, Hold on to your partner's arm.

Page 67

Ex 2	1. Pull into a circular direction. 2. Block partner with a steering wheel motion.
Ex 3	A rearwards movement; A forwards movement.
Ex 4	O GOSHI (and many others...)

"STARDUST" ANSWERS

Page 69
The hold-down counts, so carry on gripping, until the referee calls out "MATTE!"
Begin fighting, so take a grip hold and throw.
Hold down broken, so try to create a hold down again.

Page 71
Ex 1   O GOSHI can be thrown from a circular movement just like the HARAI GOSHI, and is, like this one, a hip throw (elastic knees, pull of the arm = look at your watch, eyes follow direction of the pull of the hand).

Ex 2   1 = O SOTO GARI
2 = HARAI GOSHI
In both throws you end up standing on one leg balanced up.

Ex 3   1 = HARAI GOSHI
2 = TAI OTOSHI
Similarities: Turning-in technique.
Differences: 1 = End up standing on one leg balanced up, grab round the hips.
2 = Blocking leg stretched out, elbow under the shoulder with a straight wrist, blocking leg is weighted.

Page 73
Ex 1   SOTO = outside (round past your partner).
UCHI = inside (between your partner's legs).
Ex 2   KO = small (inside muscles of the thigh tensed).
O = large (outside muscles of the thigh tensed).
Ex 3   1 = O SOTO GARI
2 = KO SOTO GAKE
Similarities: UKE's leg is attacked from the outside.
Differences: 1 = Sweep and end up standing on one leg balanced up.
2 = Hook your leg in from the outside.

Page 75
Ex 2   Pull the arm, 'T' step, keep pulling, go down low, sweep through from 12 to 3 o'clock, leg is an extension of the hips, arm pushes downwards.
Ex 4   Take a grip-hold.

Page 77
Ex 2   Pull the arm, 'T' step, sweep with the sole of the foot, leg stretched out, arms push downwards.

"STARDUST" ANSWERS

Page 79
Ex 1 Lapel hand (right) pulls towards your shoulder.
Left hand pushes his elbow backwards and outwards (steering wheel movement).

Ex 2 With the grip (i.e. hand on UKE's arm is pulling) from a backwards movement (partner is pushing).
Here, the SASAE TSURI KOMI ASHI is thrown against the grip (i.e. high collar hand is pullling) from a circular motion.

Ex 3 1 = SASAE TSURI KOMI ASHI
2 = DE ASHI BARAI
Similarities: Both are foot techniques.
Differences: 1 = The partner's weighted leg is stopped with your own leg, high collar hand pulls.
2 = The partner's unweighted leg is swept away, high collar hand presses.

Page 83
Ex 1 If he (partner) reacts by going back: KO UCHI MAKI KOMI.
If he doesn't react: KOSHI GURUMA, follow through with a grip hold.

Ex 2 1 = KO UCHI GARI
2 = KO UCHI MAKI KOMI
Similarities: The forward diagonal leg is reapt away.
Differences: 1 = Reap with the sole, leg stretched out, arm pushes downwards.
2 = The partner's leg is reapt away, left arm laid over partner's thigh, close contact to partner, go down with your partner as you throw.

Page 86
Ex 1 Slide well under your partner with bent leg (bottom close to heel).

Ex 2 Arms pull partner hard into you, control his fall and roll over without letting go and start a grip hold at once.

Ex 3 High collar grip. You push, your partner pushes back. Or: Partner pushes hard and you are going backwards.

Page 90
Ex 1 TOMOE NAGE: In the YOKO TOMOE NAGE, you lie crosswise in front of your partner.

Ex 2 Pull sideways

Ex 3 KO UCHI BARAI.

Ex 4 Russian lift, JUJI GATAME

175

"STARDUST" ANSWERS

S. 92
Ex 2 Bringing your arms together, lift your partner, then do a steering wheel movement.
Ex 3 1 = OKURI ASHI BARAI
2 = DE ASHI BARAI
Similarities: Foot techniques (leg swept away), steering wheel movement.
Differences: 1 = Both legs are swept away.
2 = One leg is swept away.

Page 94
Ex 2 1 = HARAI GOSHI
2 = KOSHI UCHI MATA
Similarities: Hip techniques balancing on one leg.
Differences: 1 = Leg is swept away to the outside.
2 = Leg is swept away through partner's legs.

Page 96
1 = Jigoro Kano
2 = Japanese Knight
3 = Self-control; show your partner courtesy; techniques and "physical intelligence".

Page 98
Ex 1 Phase 2 – Go down low, step round him (dodge); if you don't go down low, you will be thrown by your partner using a hip technique.
Ex 2 Pull forwards for a hip technique, partner reacts backwards, follow up with a TANI OTOSHI.
Ex 3 1 = TANI OTOSHI
2 = KO UCHI MAKI KOMI
Similarities: In both techniques you fall with your partner, you can use both if your partner reacts backwards to your pull, in order to dodge the expected hip technique.
Differences: 1 = Arm pushes against the chest, roller skate step.
2 = Left arm laid over the partners thigh, partner's leg is reapt away.

Page 100
Ex 1 TOMOE NAGE, YOKO TOMOE NAGE
Ex 2 MA SUTEMI WAZA = TOMOE NAGE

"STARDUST" ANSWERS

	YOKO SUTEMI WAZA = YOKO TOMOE NAGE, YOKO OTOSHI
Ex 3	UKI WAZA (Rearwards pulled fall): TORI's stretched-out leg is not placed to the side. It is placed cross-wise in front of partner, who falls straight forward over it. In the YOKO SUTEMI WAZA, UKE is standing crosswise to partner and falls to his side.

Page 102
Ex 1	Partner well bent over.
Ex 2	1 = TOMOE NAGE
	2 = SUMI GAESHI
	Similarities: MA SUTEMI WAZA
	Differences: 1 = High collar grip, foot in his groin.
	2 = Grip right down partner's back, foot onto the inside of his upper leg.
Ex 3	MA SUTEMI WAZA
Ex 4	Like a ball you tumble over with your partner finally landing on top of him and taking him into a grip hold.

Page 104
Ex 1	Phase 4 - bring bent leg to the inside of thigh, then sweep upwards moving like a spring.
Ex 2	1 = KOSHI UCHI MATA
	2 = HANE GOSHI
	Similarities: One-legged hip technique, balance on leg.
	Differences: 1 = Stretched-out sweeping leg.
	2 = Bent leg is placed in position and is first stretched later as you balance up on the one leg.
Ex 3	HANE GOSHI, KOSHI UCHI MATA, O GOSHI, TSURI KOMI GOSHI, KOSHI GURUMA, HARAI GOSHI.

Page 105
SASAE TSURI KOMI ASHI, SUMI GAESHI, TAI OTOSHI, UCHI MATA, O GOSHI, IPPON SEOI NAGE, KO UCHI BARAI, O SOTO GARI.

Page 107
Ex 1	1 = ASHI UCHI MATA: Your standing leg is on the outside, leg to be attacked on the lapel hand side.
	2 = KOSHI UCHI MATA: Standing leg is between partner's legs, leg to be attacked is on the leading arm side.

177

"STARDUST" ANSWERS

Ex 2 KEN-KEN UCHI MATA; If your partner doesn't go down at first attempt, hop as you stand in the balanced position while at the same time continuing to pull and push.
YOKO SUMI GAESHI (if partner reacts backwards).

Ex 3 KO UCHI GARI reap, forwards, backwards, sideways and circular.

Page 109

Ex 1 Phase 2 - Use a large step forwards, upper body upright in order to grip the partner's thigh, head ducks under the partner's arm.

Ex 2 KHABARELLI, SASAE TSURI KOMI ASHI

Ex 3 1 = O UCHI GARI
2 = O UCHI GARI (with pulling one leg of the ground by hand)
Similarities: The forward leg on the same side of the partner is attacked.
Differences: 1 = Lapel grip.
2 = Grasp round the thigh.

Page 111

Ex 1 Arm pulls leg in an arc, one lapel is pulled down.

Ex 2 KATA ASHI DORI, IPPON SEOI NAGE, SEOI OTOSHI, KO UCHI MAKI KOMI, DE ASHI BARAI.

Ex 3 1 = O UCHI GARI (with pulling one leg off the ground by hand)
2 = KATA ASHI DORI
Similarities: One leg pulled away.
Differences: 1 = Standing leg is pulled away, then O UCHI GARI.
2 = Forward leg pulled in an arc.

Page 113

Ex 1 Block the knee with the hand, in order to press your partner over.
KUKICHI TAOSHI = Push a dead tree over.

Ex 2 1 = KUKICHI TAOSHI
2 = KATA ASHI DORI
Similarities: The leg is grasped.
Differences: 1 = Knee is blocked, partner is pushed over.
2 = Leg is pulled in an arc so that the partner falls down.

Ex 3 Lead into a KO UCHI GARI, however then grasp the attacked leg and block it while you push the partner over.

"STARDUST" ANSWERS

Page 115
Ex 1   Hip technique ones.
Ex 2   Hips low down and forwards (countering the partner's throwing direction) = blocking.
Ex 3   Lifting: Drop down low, push forward with the stomach, stretch your legs to an upright position.

Page 117
Ex 1   Phase 1: Blocking.
Ex 2   Blocking – Hips low and forwards.
Lifting – Stomach out and forwards, lift from the knees.
Throwing – Push the hip forward over which you will swing your partner.
Ex 3   1 = USHIRO GOSHI
2 = UTSURI GOSHI
Similarities: Blocking: Hips low and forwards.   Block partner: Hips forward; both throws are counters.
Differences: 1 = After blocking, partner is pushed over.
2 = After blocking, partner is first of all swung round.

Page 120
Ex 1   1 = TE GURUMA
2 = O UCHI GARI (with pulling one leg of the ground by hand)
Similarities: Grasp partner's thigh round from the outside.
Differences: 1 = Leading leg supports the lifting movement.
2 = Reaping leg reaps and the standing leg is pulled away by hand.
Ex 2   Pull the elbows down, wait for the counter reaction, push the arm up, duck under his arm with your head and your arm.
Ex 3   Lift up from the knees, stomach and hips forward, upper body upright, leg can provide support.

Page 122
Ex 1   1 = TE GURUMA
2 = TE GURUMA as a counter to SEOI NAGE
Similarities: Hand grasps partner's thigh in order to lift him.
Differences: 1 = Hand grasps the thigh from the outside attacking movement.
2 = Hand grasps the thigh through the legs from behind – counter movement.

179

"STARDUST" ANSWERS

Ex 2   TANI OSHI against a hip technique.
Ex 3   Stomach and hips pushed forwards, lift up from the legs.

Page 125

Ex 1   PULLING OUT sequence: UKE is pushing hard – go backwards to the right and turn foot in – Charlie Chaplin sequence – right foot forward.
KODOKAN rearwards: UKE is pushing lightly – go backwards to the right and turn foot in – left foot in a tight half-circle backwards – right foot forward.
KODOKAN forwards: UKE is pulling – T-step – left foot round in a half-circle –- right foot forward.
Straight Sequence: Go sideways – heel forwards.

Ex 2   GURUMA = Wheel (partner goes over in a cartwheel).
TE GURUMA, ASHI GURUMA, O GURUMA, KATA GURUMA, YOKO GURUMA, KOSHI GURUMA, HIZA GURUMA.

Ex 3   1 = HARAI GOSHI
2 = ASHI GURUMA
Similarities: Partner is thrown over the lifting leading leg from outside.
Differences: 1 = Leg sweeps, hand grasps round the hips.
2 = Leading leg lies diagonally in front of the partner, who is pushed over the leg in a wheeling action. High collar grip, or lapel grip.

Page 128

Ex 1   1 = ASHI UCHI MATA
2 = O GURUMA
Similarities: Standing leg swept outside your partner's leg.
Differences: 1 = Leg is swept on the side of your lapel hand.
2 = The leading leg lies diagonally in front of the partner's thigh (like a level crossing barrier).

Ex 2   Starting sequence like O SOTO GARI, rearward leading leg held behind the partner's thigh and partner pulled diagonally over it and pushed down.

Page 132

Ex 1   Partner pulled sharply forwards so that he has to step forwards.
Ex 2   Lapel Grips, SEOI NAGE on the knees.
Ex 3   Grasp the leg and push over backwards.

Page 133

Ex 1   1 = TE GURUMA against a SEOI NAGE

"STARDUST" ANSWERS

2 = KATA GURUMA (Standing)
Similarities: Lift up from the knees, stomach and hips forward.
Differences: 1 = Grasp partner's thigh round from the outside.
2 = Grasp partner's thigh round from the inside.

Ex 2 So that you don't damage your spine: The power derived from the legs can be used better, besides, so that you can correctly achieve a tipping movement forwards.

Ex 3 Phase 3 - Pull the arm, drop down bending the knees, grasp the partner's thigh (neck makes contact with partner's thigh) straighten the back.

Page 135

Ex 1 Pull the partner's arm upwards (left), the other hand (right) traps the arm from above, right hand moves towards your left foot.

Ex 2 1 = KO UCHI MAKI KOMI
2 = SOTO MAKI KOMI
Similarities: Both throws are techniques where you go down with your partner (MAKI KOMI).
Differences: 1 = Grasp partner's thigh, reaping leg from the inside.
2 = Trap the arm, blocking leg on the outside.

Ex 3 1 = TAI OTOSHI
2 = SOTO MAKI KOMI
Similarities: Blocking leg pulled in close to partner.
Differences: 1 = Elbow presses up under the shoulder, wrist held straight, throw by lifting and turning.
2 = Trap the arm from above, throw by going down with your partner.

Page 138

Ex 1 KOSHI GURUMA, O GOSHI, HARAI GOSHI, KOSHI UCHI MATA, HANE GOSHI

Ex 2 Partner falls on top of you; that is a score for your opponent in a contest.

Ex 3 You will, otherwise, land on your back next to your partner; that is a possible score for the opponent in a contest.

Page 140

Ex 1 Your partner turns to do a hip technique. If he stays upright: TANI OTOSHI, URA NAGE. If he bends forward: YOKO GURUMA.
You follow up with a grip hold.

181

"STARDUST" ANSWERS

Ex 2   1 = TANI OTOSHI
       2 = YOKO GURUMA
       Similarities: Counter techniques against hip techniques.
       Differences: 1 = Glide backwards.
                          2 = Glide forwards and inwards.

Page 144

Ex 2   Step over as in the TSUBAME GAESHI (lower leg up high), and then do a SASAE TSURI KOMI ASHI yourself.

Page 148

Ex 1   Pull the diagonal arm across your body.
       Grab far down the partner's back, pull in close, place weight on his shoulder.
       Using the grip down his back pull partner down sideways.

Ex 2   1 = YOKO SUMI GAESHI
       2 = SUMI GAESHI
       Similarities: SUTEMI WAZA.
       Differences: 1 = YOKO SUTEMI WAZA – arm pulls sideways, leg placed diagonally.
                          2 = MA SUTEMI WAZA – hand pulls past partner's head, leg stretched out straight.

Ex 3   After a failed ASHI UCHI MATA you jump into a YOKO SUMI GAESHI. Your lifting leg becomes your reaping leg without being placed down on the ground as you go.

Page 149

Ex 1   1 = KHABARELLI
       2 = ASHI UCHI MATA
       Similarities: Standing with leg balanced upwards.
       Differences: 1 = Backwards balanced position.
                          2 = Forwards balanced position.

Ex 2   Try UCHI MATA, partner reacts rearwards, follow up with an O UCHI GARI, partner now reacts forwards, follow up with a KHABARELLI, if the partner now tries to keep standing, you can follow up by going into an UCHI MATA.

Ex 3   Grasp the arm on the same side as the grasping hand, pull down on the elbows, cross over grip.
       Grip diagonally across, pass the arm on to your other hand, then grip down the back.

"STARDUST" ANSWERS

SUMI GAESHI, YOKO SUMI GAESHI, O UCHI GARI, ASHI UCHI MATA, KOSHI UCHI MATA

Page 152

Ex 1   1 = SEOI NAGE
       2 = KOGA SEOI NAGE
       Similarities: Shoulder throw.
       Differences: 1 = Arm grips from inside and locks.
                       2 = Arm grips from outside and locks. (A SEOI NAGE turned into from the outside).

Ex 2   Free the grip with your right hand, left hand held under his arm, grasp his arm with your right hand (see 'Breaking the lapel grip' on Page 20).

Ex 3   IPPON SEOI NAGE, MOROTE SEOI NAGE, SEOI NAGE (on the knees).

Page 154

Ex 1   YOKO SUTEMI WAZA

Ex 2   If, when you start an ASHI UCHI MATA, your partner reacts by moving backwards, follow up with a YOKO GAKE; if he moves forwards use an ASHI UCHI MATA.

183

Martial Arts

MEYER & MEYER SPORT

Ulrich Klocke
Judo – Top Action
Illustrated book

Spectacular photographs show the best judo techniques in standing position and on the ground. The author has selected the most successful throws from e.g. World Championships and Olympic Games. Putting these sequences into a specific order, the ambitious judo fighter is able to improve his individual techniques.

170 pages
Full-colour print
About 600 photos
Hardcover, 22,5 x 28,5 cm
ISBN 1-84126-035-5
£ 22.95 UK/$ 34.- US/
$ 49.95 CDN/€ 27.90

If you are interested in Meyer & Meyer Sport and our large programme, please visit us **online** or call our **Hotline** ▼

online:
▶ www.m-m-sports.com

Hotline:
▶ ++49 (0)1 80 / 5 10 11 15

We are looking forward to your call!

Please order our catalogue!

MEYER & MEYER Verlag | Von-Coels-Straße 390 | D-52080 Aachen, Germany | Fax +49 (0)2 41-9 58 10-10